D0358557

The Watered Garden

GOSPEL FOLIO PRESS
P. O. Box 2041, Grand Rapids MI 49501-2041
Available in the UK from
JOHN RITCHIE LTD., Kilmarnock, Scotland

Originally published in *Counsel, Food for the Flock,* and *Uplook* magazines.

Cover photo by Dan Spoelstra, Spoelstra Studios, Grand Rapids, MI
Cover flowers from Eastern Floral, Grand Rapids, MI
Cover and book design by J. B. Nicholson, Jr.

Photo credits: Doug Dixon, p. 58; Boyd Nicholson, pp. 16-17, 48-49, 76-77, 82, 95;
J. B. Nicholson, Jr., pp. 10, 21, 27, 37, 54, 64, 89; Marilyn Pell, pp. 32, 44; Dan Spoelstra, p. 71.

Copyright © 1993
J. Boyd Nicholson
All Rights Reserved

Co-published by
Counsel Magazine, P. O. Box 427, St. Catharines, ON L2R 6V9
and by
Gospel Folio Press, P. O. Box 2041, Grand Rapids, MI 49501-2041

Printed in the United States of America

For Him

Ere He, from chaos, order brought,
The Saviour thought—
On me.
Not thoughts of vengeance or of wrath,
When stars began their fiery path,
But thoughts of love—
For me.

Not robed with light or burning flame,
The Saviour came—
For me.
But in the very form of man,
With hands that worked and eyes that ran
With tears—
For me.

The very night He was betrayed,
The Saviour prayed—
For me.
'Twas not for gold or painless lot,
A greater wealth for me He sought,
His joy fulfilled—
In me.

Then up Golgotha's bleak ascent,
The Saviour went—
For me.
No backward glance, no look of hate,
As there, beyond old Salem's gate
God's judgment bore—
For me.

"For me, for me," Is there one thing
The Saviour wants—
From me?
"Thy heart, thy heart, I want it all."
Ah! Lord, before those pierced feet I fall.
Can I withhold—
From Thee?

"And the Lord shall guide thee continually,
and satisfy thy soul in drought . . . and thou shalt be like a watered garden,
and like a spring of water, whose waters fail not."

Isaiah 58:11

Contents

Foreword

Seldom does one have the dubious honour of editing an editor. It is especially sobering when the author was the one who taught you how to speak your native tongue! Yet I do take it to be a high privilege to work on the publication of this book, and happily offer these lines as some small deposit on a very large debt.

A book of this style has three great benefits. It is, first of all, *a book for our times.* It can be read in snatches, one page at a time if you wish. They say the best books make you lay them down—to think. This is just such a volume. It speaks to our times, times that are serious, with challenges that demand real answers. These pages move you without becoming maudlin. They give you a vision of what might be in your life by God's grace, without being simply visionary. The collection is very much a garden of ideas, full of variety, carefully weeded, redolent with the fragrance of the Master.

Secondly, it is *a book that was written over time.* You can tell as you read these pages that the essays and poems were not plucked from the garden all at once. They came, not from the need to meet publisher's deadlines, but out of the multifarious circumstances of life. You may find yourself smiling one moment, blinking back a tear the next, but the book will not leave you untouched. And you will be left with the impression as you turn its last page that, to the author, these things are real. But it is not the author's purpose that you might know him better through his writing, but that you know *Him* better.

Thirdly, *the subject of the book is timeless.* It does not waste itself on momentary doctrinal fads or passing fancies. When you deal with the Book of books, when you speak of the King of kings, when, by faith, you enter the Holy of holies, you are in the presence of things eternal. No matter your age or maturity in the things of God, you will find ample here to set your mind to meditating and your heart to singing.

There are two ways to hold an audience: you can settle for novelty, or you can invest the time to be able to present orthodoxy in a fresh way. This is the need of the hour. And what is the secret of this freshness? It is an appetite for all that God has for us. It is an unwillingness to be satisfied with the mediocre.

When I was a child, it was not unusual for my father to ask, as we stood viewing a sunset, "What colours would you mix, Son, to get that hue of purple along the edge of that cloud?" When high school hit, with its attendant influences, I would sometimes begin to overuse some trendy word or phrase. "I've heard that word several times today already," I would hear. "Can you think of a synonym?" Sometimes we would be asked something like, "What's the difference between 'continuous' and 'contiguous'?" Words, like a fire, could be very helpful or very harmful. As Mark Twain noted, "The difference between the right word and the almost right word is the difference between lightning and lightning-bug." This drive for the right word, for the best word, was especially important when it came to the things of God. There was no room for being sloppy or slipshod. It was worth the time to get it right, especially when one was teaching others, for teachers would have "the greater judgment."

Of course, there is more than mere wording on a page here. What good is it to have the phrase right if the spirit is not right? Far better, if one must choose, to have a tender heart than to have a sharp mind or an eloquent tongue (1 Cor. 13). Thankfully, such a choice is not necessary if both heart and mind, word and deed are subject to the Lord.

The following pages—for the most part as magazine articles in their original form—have already been graciously used by the Spirit to bring solace to the sorrowing, encouragement to the disheartened, and redirection of our gaze toward the Saviour. May He also use this more permanent edition "to edification, exhortation, and comfort" that, like watered gardens, our lives may be full of fruit and fragrance for Him. *"Awake, O north wind; and come, thou south; blow upon my garden, that the spices thereof may flow out. Let my Beloved come into His garden, and eat His pleasant fruits"* (Song of Sol. 4:16).

J. B. Nicholson, Jr.
September, 1993
Grand Rapids, Michigan

The Garden and the Spring

It was over forty years ago, and I was young, but I have never forgotten the pleasant experience of the day. It was blistering hot and the Bunder Road was long and uncomfortably crowded as I made my way into the Indian city. Unexpectedly I saw a little gate on the other side of the road, with a wrought iron inscription: "Mahatma Ghandi Gardens." Crossing the busy street, I passed through the gate and found myself in a most delightful little garden, as the sign had promised, walled in from the busyness outside.

Strangely enough, though so near to such a well-used thoroughfare, I was alone there. Not even a gardener was in sight. Finding a bench in the shade of a fragrant tree, I just sat back and soaked up the relief this little sanctuary provided. Water, sprayed on the grass, had kept it unusually green in the hot Indian summer. The plants too were glistening with moisture. The air was heavy with the sweet fragrance of many blossoms. Orchids nestled in the branches of tropical trees. The sound of the water bubbling here and spraying there was almost as refreshing as a shower bath. Birds chirped contentedly and flew from branch to branch.

There are few places of respite so pleasant as a watered garden. This is the picture of the human soul as the Lord desires it to be. We read this in Isaiah 58:11. The people to whom those words were addressed were beautiful in many ways. Certainly the Lord thought so. He gave them a generous approbation and testified to five outstanding qualities which He appreciated in them. Their habits were right; the Lord said that they sought His presence daily. Their desires were right for they delighted to know God's path clearly. Their position was right for they followed God's pattern carefully. Their prayers were right, for they asked for God's purposes religiously. Their pleasures were right for they delighted in their pursuit of God personally (v. 2).

But something was not right. They knew it, and God knew it. They were missing the sense of the smile of God upon them (v. 3). They seemed correct in everything, but they were remiss in some significant areas of their lives. They were theologically correct, they were positionally right, but they were sadly remiss in the practical application of what they knew.

Outside the door of their complacency sat those bound in sin, burdened with sorrow, bereft in poverty, and begging for a loaf of bread. Some of them perhaps were their own children (vv. 6-7).

Inside, they were discussing theological niceties that cost them absolutely nothing. They were proud of their "fasting," the things they "gave up for the Lord" (vv. 3-4). Little wonder that the Lord called His servant to "Cry aloud, spare not, lift up thy voice like a trumpet." Hopefully his call would penetrate their comfortable apathy before it was too late for the lost out there in the desperate dark.

That was not all the Lord had to say. There were three things that had to go (v. 9). They must remove the yoke of unlawful communion. The unequal yoke is painful to both partners and the only answer is not adjustment, but removal. The unequal yoke is not a matter of *contact*. We meet the world every day (so we need the basin every day!). It is a matter of *contract*, being bound by love, loyalty, or law to that which is alien to a life of fellowship with God. The marriage yoke, however, is fastened by a higher law, and God's intent was that death alone would break it.

They must withdraw the finger of unkind criticism. How easy to join in the assassination by tongue, of the character of some absent person—if not by serious allegation, then by nodding, silent assent. All our ecclesiastical accuracy, all our theological brilliance, all our golden eloquence, all our zealous activity is made a mockery, by a single finger pointed in the wrong direction, manward instead of Godward.

They must silence the tongue of unprofitable conversation. Vain words are "unemployed" words. They are idle, not accomplishing anything of value. Mouths rattling away with useless palaver. They need not be dirty or evil, just nothing worthwhile. How many of us tremble a little at the thought of having to give account to the Lord Himself for every idle word? James is the one who can convict us about the tongue. "A fire," he says, "a world of iniquity," defiling the body and starting up the wheels of lust whose axles are ignited by infernal heat (Jas. 3:6).

If those people would, and if all of us will obey this urgent cry, then our souls will be fragrant, refreshing, and fruitful as is a watered garden. They will be sweet, and satisfying to others, as sacrificial as an unfailing spring that ever gives out from hidden resources.

"Lord, save us from cold forms of things that blind the heavenly view,
And make our souls like bubbling springs and gardens wet with dew."

So Rich a Crown

He came, out from God, a gift from the Father's heart. Descending from the throne high and lifted up, He laid aside the garments of His majesty. The train of that robe of light filled the heavenly sanctuary with its radiance. Stepping down from the infinities of uncreated light, He passed through the creature realms of wondering angels, taking nothing of them. Still downward He came to one of the billions of His galaxies which He Himself had made. There His destination hung, a speck of sunlit stardust, so insignificant among gigantic suns and island universes that only He could find it, for in the eternal purposes of love and grace He had placed it there as a paradise for His creature man.

He arrived on the dark side of the planet, for it was night where He appeared. Yet that darkness must give way and bow to the effulgence of God. The night sky blazed with glory. A multitude of angels heralded God's praise in the heavens and man's privilege and prospects on earth. Blessed creatures indeed all they of the human race! The Son of God had come to earth to bring heaven into their hearts and them into heaven at last. Though full well He knew the price His love would pay to make it so.

What a story of the glory of God on earth, walking, working, weeping, among His creatures. Oh, how they would welcome this visitor of love and sweetness to this sordid world of tears and pain that man had made out of the paradise of God! Ah, sad and shameful is the record. He came, but there was no room for Him. They wanted His bread in their mouths, but not His beneficent rule in their hearts. They wanted His healing powers, but not His holy claims. They were filled with wonder at His grace, but filled with wrath at His truth.

At last their hatred exceeded. They must find Him and destroy Him. His radiance had exposed their sins. Their insect consciences scurried for cover. They mocked at His meekness and scorned His compassion for sinners. They had made their decision. The darkness they loved and therefore the light they must extinguish.

Gethsemane! So they found Him at the garden of the oil press . . . on the dark side of the planet. In the night He had prayed in agony till His sweat, like great blood drops, fell to the ground. He had seen what none else but God could see. He had surveyed "the place afar off" where none else but He would go, and He bowed to the Father's will. He stood before their rabble mob, Holiness personified. Love was His banner and compassion the beating of His heart, even for those who hated Him without a cause. His body bathed in the sweat of His anguish and the traitor's kiss still wet upon His cheek, they led Him away to the judgment of men.

Gabbatha! The soldiers gathered round in raucous glee. "A King?" they mocked, "Then anoint Him," and they spat in His lovely face. "A King? Then give Him a robe," and they threw around His bleeding back a soldier's cloak. "A King? Then give Him a staff of authority" and they put a brittle reed into His hand. "A King? Then give Him a crown," and they pressed a crown of thorns upon His blessed brow. "A King? Then He must have a throne," and they took Him to Golgotha. There they nailed Him through His hands and feet to the only throne men ever gave Him.

Yet out of this race of sinners they have come by the millions. From habitations of cruelty and homes of respectability, from hell-holes of ignorance and halls of learning. Still they come! His cross, His suffering love, has won their hearts. His beauty has captured their affections. He is to them the Altogether Lovely One. They are His and He is theirs by eternal decree. Is it any wonder that, by faith, they gather around Him week by week and show forth His death, remembering with sweetest sadness the giving of His body and the shedding of His precious blood and looking forward "till He come."

> *When I survey the wondrous cross on which the Prince of glory died,*
> *My richest gain I count but loss, and pour contempt on all my pride.*
>
> *Forbid it, Lord, that I should boast save in the Cross of Christ, my God;*
> *All the vain things that charm me most I sacrifice them to His blood.*
>
> *See from His head, His hands, His feet, sorrow and love flow mingled down;*
> *Did e'er such love and sorrow meet, or thorns compose so rich a crown?*
>
> *Were the whole realm of nature mine, that were an offering far too small;*
> *Love so amazing, so divine, demands my heart, my life, my all!*
> —Isaac Watts

The Golden Lock of Hair

The little blue tin was hardly ever seen. Usually it came out of the drawer in the fall of the year. Inside was a string of children's beads. Nothing valuable nor special about them in any way, save only, that fastened in the cord of the beads was one lock of golden red hair.

The Christian lady told me about it one day. Her little girl, Helen, or Ella as they called her, was playing with the beads and somehow got them tangled in her hair. Try as they might, they could not unloose them. So at last the mother took the scissors and cut off the lock of hair. She kept that string of children's beads, and the lock of hair still fastened to it, in the little blue tin that I had seen.

Ella was a beautiful child, I learned, with a sweet and gentle nature, the joy of her young mother and father. She took seriously ill and in those days little was understood about her malady. Radical surgery was performed to save her life but at the tender age of four the Lord took her away Home out of what would have been a life of suffering.

The grief and sorrow of the loss of such a lovely little flower can only be appreciated by those who have passed that way. The young father, though a believer in Christ, became bitter and angry with God at the loss of his little darling and in such a way. The wee girl was buried in an unmarked grave and never in his life did the father return to it. He seldom spoke of his Ella and then only with difficulty. The years passed by and when he was seventy he said to me, "I know that I'm truly saved but I have nothing for God. I shall be saved as by fire." Though personally I know there was many a cup of water given along the way that shall not lose its reward.

The mother carried the wound of that loss in her heart right to the grave, but she bowed to the Father's will and out of the furnace of sorrow she came forth as gold and in her quiet way became a minister of comfort to many with the comfort wherewith she herself had been comforted of God.

We all must pass through deep waters at some time in life. For some the waters are deeper and darker than for others but it is the inevitable lot of human experience. In Isaiah 43:2, it is "when" not "if". We all must pass that way sometime. But it is "through" not "into" for the waters of trial are not for our *destruction* but for our *instruction*. If by the grace and help of God we can bow to Him in the sorrow we will come forth as gold. If we rebel, despise His chastening or faint under the rod, we will not bear the peaceable fruit of righteousness (Hebrews. 12), and we can suffer loss at the judgment seat of Christ.

The years have passed. The mother and father have both been re-united in glory with their darling daughter (2 Sam. 12:23). A lock of hair, be it ever so golden, was not much to be left with, but it was all part of the treasure of memories and the token of hope that one day they would be together again beyond this vale of tears.

After some searching, I found that unmarked baby grave one day in a shaded, overgrown corner of a cemetery in Scotland, and stood alone with my thoughts and prayers, too personal to share with any but the Lord. That grave and that golden lock of hair have had a lesson for me in my life that I hope I shall not easily forget.

Ella, you see, was my sister.

Jesus, Lover of my soul, let me to Thy bosom fly
While the billows near me roll, while the tempest still is high:
Hide me, O my Saviour, hide, till the storm of life is past;
Safe into the haven guide, O receive my soul at last.

Other refuge have I none; hangs my helpless soul on Thee;
Leave, ah! leave me not alone, still support and comfort me.
All my hope on Thee is stayed, all my help from Thee I bring;
Cover my defenseless head with the shadow of Thy wing.

Plenteous grace with Thee is found, grace to pardon all my sin;
Let the healing streams abound; make and keep me pure within.
Thou of life the fountain art; freely let me take of Thee;
Spring Thou up within my heart now and to eternity. —Charles Wesley

Every Tongue Confess

She has never spoken a word nor heard a sound in her life. Abandoned as a child, she spent most of her first eight years in a crib. She was found and taken in to be loved and cared for by an attending nurse. At last the authorities acted and, they said, because of the "religious influence" she was under, she had to be removed from the nurse's home. All contact was lost for about 14 years. Through those long years, faithful prayer was made that this poor, needy girl may be found again. Then one day, in a local park, there she was—poor, unkempt, living alone, abused, and angry at God that she could neither hear nor speak.

The nurse, now married, took this poor, young woman home where she and her doctor husband loved and cared for her. Of course, they had one great longing—that she might discover that the God she angrily rejected, really loved her and had given His Son to die for her that her soul might be saved.

These friends, in love for her, had saved her physically from a life of grief and deprivation. Perhaps by this she might learn of that great love of God, ready and willing to save her soul from eternal sorrow and loss. Then one day, after much struggling, the light of the gospel shone into her heart and in simple faith she received the Saviour.

My colleague in the gospel and I were preaching where she lived, and a baptism for new believers was arranged. There she was! About to step into the water and declare her love for the Lord Jesus. By sign language she understood what to do. After reading a paper containing her story to the assembled audience, the baptizing brother asked aloud the question, "Have you believed on the Lord Jesus Christ as your personal Saviour?" The question was passed to her in sign language as she stood in the water. At once her face broke into a radiant smile and she signalled enthusiastically, "Yes!" and the only sound she can make burst from her lips. We could not hold back the tears.

We had just finished preaching the gospel for over an hour, but that young lady communicated more by that single sound than all the words we had spoken. We could only hear an unusual sound from her throat, but all heaven was witness to it, and, translated into heaven's language, surely it would bring glory to the Lord Jesus.

We choked as we tried to sing:

"Not a burden we bear,
Not a sorrow we share,
But our toil He doth richly repay;
Not a grief nor a loss,
Not a frown nor a cross,
But is blest if we trust and obey." [1]

It is easy to sing about losses and crosses when we are sitting in comfort and surrounded by the multiplied evidences of the beneficence of God. Here was a young lady who has known suffering and a significant loss in her life, yet through the love of Christ, made real to her by the faithful prayers and tenderness of those who cared, at last her embattled spirit yielded to that wondrous love.

Today she is a shining witness to her Saviour—and to the persevering love of those who would not let her go.

---

1. Words by J. H. Sammis

The Name of Jesus

Illustrious Name! Deserving veneration,
But two brief syllables in every tongue,
O speak with reverential intonation
By lisping child or ancient's song,
The Name of Jesus!

Yea, taste as fruit this sweetest Appellation,
That all its succulence may fill the soul,
O sing with musical reverberation,
That we may echo clear from pole to pole
The Name of Jesus!

Yet think, afar, in darkest habitation,
In desert solitude or where the wicked dwell,
A man like me, who longs for consolation,
And yet upon whose ears there never fell
The Name of Jesus!

Then who will go with Heaven's declaration
Of God, whose love is from eternal days?
Who gave His Son to death's humiliation
That souls, forgiv'n, shall ever sing and praise
The Name of Jesus!

Influenza

Doctors warned that it was coming and that the elderly, especially, should be inoculated against it. Another powerful strain of influenza was making its way from the Orient. So it has happened in our country as predicted. From coast to coast, thousands have been laid low with this elusive and invasive virus. Our local hospital was closed to all but essential visitors. Some school classes had two-thirds absenteeism because of the widespread sickness. Most of us have been hit by it. The question is frequently asked, "Have you had the flu yet?"

Influenza! It is a fact, however, that every single one of us has "Influenza" every day of our lives. "Influenza" is really just Italian for "influence" and we all have an influence of some kind, one upon the other.

You would have thought that the children of Israel would all have been glad to cross Jordan at last and enter the Land of Promise to taste its milk and honey. They were, of course. At least, all excepting the tribes of Gad and Reuben. As they viewed the green pastures of Jazer in the land of Gilead, east of the Jordan, they saw that it was "a place for cattle" (Num. 32:1). They went to Moses with the request that they not go over the Jordan with the rest, but remain there with their herds. They said—and we can almost hear their emphasis— "And we have cattle."

Moses was angry. He reminded them of their fathers, Shammua and Geuel, who, forty years before, had returned with the other spies bearing a negative report of the land of God's promise. They had "discouraged the heart of the children of Israel." This bad influence on the people had wrought dire results of long wandering and widespread death. Now here were their children at it again. Moses was plain and straight to the point, "Wherefore discourage ye the heart of the children of Israel?" They were more concerned about their own interests than the general blessing of the people. The cattle meant more than the battle, and they cared little about the serious negative influence they had on the children of Israel.

It is not insignificant that when the Lord Jesus cast out the legion of demons from the wild man of Gadara, and permitted them to enter the swine which ran into the sea, the people violently objected and begged the Lord to leave their territory. They were the GAD-arenes, descendants of the same children of Gad of long ago. They would rather have had their pigs back and the devil for a neighbour than the presence of the lovely Son of God among them! It is surely a most solemn thing to have such a critical spirit and such a negative attitude. It soon influences our children and will reap the same bitter fruit in their lives.

Involved with Gad and Reuben in their discouraging influence was also half the tribe of Manasseh. These also wanted their inheritance outside of the land of promise (but nearby). Again it is significant that we read the record of the king, Manasseh, that he "seduced [the children of Israel] to do more evil than did the nations whom the Lord destroyed . . ." His influence was one that caused the people to sin. He was held accountable, not only for the sins he committed, but also for the sins he caused others to commit.

We, in our day, are warned in the New Testament not to provoke our children to wrath. If we do so, we may confess that sin and be forgiven, but we have no power to deal with the sin we have caused our children to commit nor to halt a process which we may begin in their lives.

In God's assembly, we all have "influenza." We influence the Lord's people in one way or the other. Because of the intimacy of that fellowship, and the fact that we are one bread and one body in the Lord, an integral part of one and another's spiritual lives, we either contribute to the health and welfare of the whole, or we are a negative hindrance by our low spiritual influence. That is why the disciplines of 1 Corinthians 11 are so severe. If one should continually be a negative influence and a hindrance to the worship and the work of the assembly by disobedience and a lack of self-judgment, the Lord will deal with that one by a temporary isolation, a weakness. Or more severely, a longer period, by sickness. In a most severe case, a permanent removal, the sleep of death will deal with that hindering influence.

Cain asked, "Am I my brother's keeper?" The answer is clear: "Yes, indeed!" How is your "influenza" today? Have you discouraged the saints, a servant of the Lord, a child of God, your own partner, your children? Have we influenced another to sin by our demeanor, our dress, our demands? Have we had an influence for God and for good upon the saints, the beloved of the Lord, inspiring them to holier and happier things? Or are we a hindering influence to their worship and work by our unspiritual attitudes?

The wise among the saints are likened to the stars. May our influence among them be like the "sweet influences of Pleiades" (Job 38:31) which cannot be bound.

The Lord Led Me

An earnest young man told the writer some time ago that the Lord had led him to come to a certain assembly to be a "pastor-teacher" there. He had recently graduated from a Bible school and felt that God had given him the gift of the teacher. I believed that he sincerely wanted some help and another point of view regarding his decision.

The assembly in question had been functioning for years and was a fair size, situated in a large city. There was a body of functioning elders and a number of mature capable brethren, with varying degrees of gift. In all honesty and with a care for the young man (and for the assembly in question!), I felt I had to ask a few pointed questions. First, as to how he felt the Lord had led him in what he was doing. His answer was alarming in its naivete and amazing in its immaturity. His decision had been made largely on what he considered was a "sign from God" and his interpretation of it.

Secondly, I was interested to discover why he located himself in a prosperous, well-gifted assembly, when the whole perishing world lay before him in vast tracts of territory unoccupied by the forces of the gospel, when the Great Commission had authorized him to "Go" in simple dependence on the Lord alone. His response to this query was simply that God had never blessed any efforts he had ever made in the gospel.

I felt it might be helpful to frankly consider with him the matter of "signs" and "the leading of the Lord." While we must maintain the principle of simple faith as a way of life and shun doubts and cynicism, we must also be on guard against the wiles of the devil, whose aim is to divert the earnest soul, working against the weakness of our flesh which panders to the gratification of self-will and self-serving interests.

The problem with signs is, first, *they can be imitated by the enemy* as in Egypt before the Exodus. *They can be misinterpreted by the servant* as in the day of Job's loss. *They can be imagined by the anxious* when there is really no sign from God at all. Someone may then ask if we are never to "put out the fleece" to get some indication from God? First of all, Gideon's fleece was his idea, not God's, although God considered the frailty of His servant and responded. Secondly, the fleece was not a token of faith, but of doubt and fear. Thirdly, even after three sign-miracles, fire on the rocks, water on the fleece and water on the ground, Gideon was still not convinced and waited for yet another sign. Gideon, in that case, heard the Word of the Lord and the divine promise. When we likewise have the clear direction of God's Word, that should be enough for us.

However, the way is not always crystal clear and sometimes we must step out seemingly in the dark. How then can we know the will of God? Fortunately there are some helps given us in this important matter of "Understanding what the will of the Lord is."

First, there is *the Word of God*. We know that God will never lead us into a path that is contrary to His Word and cannot be substantiated by sound scriptural principles. It may be a popular path, long pursued by others, pleasant, applauded and supported by many, but if it contravenes biblical principles, it is not the directive will of God.

In harmony with this, there is *the indwelling Spirit of God*. If we are in fellowship with God and willing for the divine will, whatever it may be, we will be convinced by the Spirit, whose ministry includes the guidance of God's people. We must be prepared, however, for an alternative course we had not considered (or previously dismissed).

Also there is *the counsel of the spiritual among the people of God*. Often these godly men and women can see things more objectively than we, when in the throes of decisions.

Least dependable, but still of value when taken with the foregoing principles, is *the sanctified common sense God has given us* to take an intelligent view of our circumstances. Paul, in Acts 27, had enough sense of the seasonal weather to know that if they set sail then, the voyage would be dangerous.

Obedience is not selective; it is all-embracing. We must settle the question before seeking further light, whether we have done all the will of God we already know! It is unlikely that God will clearly open up step No. 2 until we have obeyed step No. 1. Willingness is not to a field of service nor a circumstance. It is an absolute willingness to the Lord Himself, without reserves, without retreat, without regard for the consequences.

If these principles are followed, we may quietly and confidently pursue that good and perfect will of God through life and be less likely to vindicate our actions later by claiming, "The Lord led me."

Remember, Reflect, Resolve

I never really understood as a boy why they had called it "Hillcrest." Our house was at the foot of the wooded hill and it was the old country road, the Green Knowe (pronounced *now*), that cut along the crest. I didn't really care about the name or how it was derived, so long as I could enjoy the wonderful benefits of living in a place that was as near to a boyish heaven as could be.

Someone, long before I was ever born, had planted an orchard there. After school, a feast of those succulent Bartletts and crisp Russets that cracked open at a bite, spoiled many a meat and potato dinner to follow. Not forgetting the challenge of trying to finish a green cooker that tightened the jaws and puckered the lips. The trees were not laid out in the orderly rows of the commercial fruit grower, but more in the spontaneity of a landscape gardener, with winding paths leading down to the stream that bordered the property. Not much of a stream really, but deep enough to carry a few small fish. Good for a lazy summer afternoon's fishing.

Then there was "the Hiding Spot" I had discovered at one place a very old tree that had resisted the erosion of the water and held the bank together in such a way as to form a small sheltered "cove."

There we were—Sheila, my devoted little fox terrier and I—sharing this haven where only the rippling of the stream made any appreciable sound. At least until I heard mother call me for dinner. She never called my name, but gave a kind of melodious "Coo-Hoo."

Whatever gets into the mind of a boy at times to make mischief I still don't really know, but that day I determined to play a trick on my mother and gave no "Coming" answer. I sat in silence to await developments. "Coo-Hoo" came the call again, a bit closer. I knew in a moment or two that she would find me. Now! I would execute my master plan! Picking up the jar of minnows, full of water, I heaved it into midstream. As it made a fair splash, I cried out in a frantic voice, "Help! Mother, help!" Mother rushed to the bank, but in doing so her foot went into a hole concealed by the long grass and she fell over with a cry of pain. She had torn a ligament in her leg.

I jumped up and ran to her as she writhed in pain. We were quite a way from the house and I did as much as a nine-year-old boy could to help her hobble, in agony, to the big chair in the corner of the front room. I was speechless. At last, she looked at me and said in her soft voice, "Son, why did you do that?" If she had only hit me on the head with a stick, I think I would have felt so much better, perhaps giving me an outlet for my remorse.

She sat in that chair for weeks, her damaged leg propped up on a stool. Every time I entered the room, I could only think, "That was my fault," and there wasn't a thing I wouldn't have done for Mother. Not an errand I would not have run, if only, if only I could show that I really did love her and grieved over my stupidity in causing her such pain.

On a good number of occasions, that incident has come to mind, especially at the end of the Lord's Supper. The bread lies broken on the table and the cup poured out and emptied. "He was wounded for our transgressions." We were the cause of all His pains. It was because of our folly and sins He suffered. We can say, "Yes, Lord, is was my fault." But do we as readily respond, as did Jonathan to David, "Whatsoever thy soul desireth, I will even do it for thee?" We may speak the words, but how deeply do they affect our lives?

Almost forty years rolled by, and with understandable anticipation, I returned to the homeland, looking forward to showing my Canadian wife and children "Hillcrest." We took the Green Knowe Road so that we could get a good view from the high side first. I felt the emotion of happy memories. Stopping at a vantage point, we got out and looked down . . . on two concrete apartment buildings plunked right in the place where the old home and the orchard once had been. Trees ripped out, winding paths all gone and the once burbling stream now a glutted ditch.

Time had carried far away the opportunities for restitution, for loving service and glad errands, at least in that context. Still, we daily have those opportunities in the circle of friends and loved ones, where we live in time today. First, not to cause them hurt and pain; and then, if possible, before it is too late, to make right where there has been wrong, and while we can "by love to serve one another." Above all, never to forget our personal responsibility in the sufferings of the Saviour. Then to resolve by God's help to show our love day by day in bringing joy to the heart of our beloved Lord through glad and willing service.

The Treasure in Earthen Vessels

2 Corinthians 4:7

Angels fain would tell the story,
Fly on beams of light to spread
News of all their Sovereign's glory,
How He lives, and once was dead.

Heavenly anthems, sounds unearthly,
Lightnings, thunders, swords of flame;
Thus could angels tell He's worthy,
And the sinner's friend proclaim.

But no angel has commission,
Not a seraph, the command:
"Preach the word of sin's remission;
Take the news to every land."

No! 'Tis left for men, forgiven—
Stammering tongue and halting thigh—
To bring news that calls to heaven
Weary souls who grieve and sigh.

But, the secret is—the glory
Must be His who died, alone;
Thus, deposits heaven's story
In clay vessels, called 'His own.'

Ah, how sad to blush and hide Him,
He who bore our sin and shame;
Silent be, while men deride Him
And the angels shout His fame.

Then let us, who know the story,
Ever ready be, though weak;
Tell His suffering and His glory,
Angels fain would fly to speak.

Who Cares?

There he lay in the gathering gloom of the hot Indian evening. Hardly discernible from the rags that partly covered him. At a glance, he almost appeared to be just another of the piles of refuse swept into a corner. Then I saw a movement. A dark, scrawny arm appeared from the rags, outstretching a hand, hopefully cupped to receive a little "baksheesh" from the passersby.

From where I was standing, a little distance away, I could barely see his face and couldn't hear his voice. It was his eyes that spoke volumes to me as I stood on that crowded city street. Sad, empty and set deep in their sockets, they spoke only of despair.

An impoverished human being, reduced to beggary. As his pleas were ignored, he withdrew under his pathetic camouflage like a frightened animal. But he is no animal. Within that taut covering of skin, within that prison cage of ribs, somewhere behind those haunting eyes there exists an eternal soul, a human spirit. A precious soul loved by God and for whom Christ died on Calvary's cross.

For a moment I tried to put my soul inside that emaciated form that knows nothing of what we in our luxuriating comfort consider to be essential for survival; someone who cares, ample food, clean water, adequate shelter, personal hygiene, and a respectable covering. I tried to look out through those eyes to see things as he might: hopeless despair, helpless fear, and a homeless future. Of course, it is most unlikely that anyone brought into the world in a land of gospel light and surrounded by prayer, Christian values and blessings, could even touch the ragged hem of the sackcloth that beggar clutched around his skin and bones, or get the feel of what living in this world means to him.

"Without Christ . . . having no hope, and without God in the world." Those words came hammering into my mind and I was profoundly convicted of having a heart from which flows so little of the love of Christ for humankind. Having eyes so seldom watered with an honest tear for the lost and perishing, my fellow-travellers to eternity.

Two men on an Indian street, but an unbridgeable gulf between them of privilege, culture, and language—at least, that was the excuse given to God as I turned to make my way back to my comfortable capsule of lodging, food and fellowship.

Fifteen thousand miles away, another scene. No beggars here. I sat waiting in a modern shopping plaza and watched the people go by. Hardly a smile creased a face. Lines of care, the tense jaw, frowns of anxiety were frequent as these shoppers walked among the glittering baubles of affluence .

Scanning those faces I became aware that the music that had been playing over the sound system had changed. The raucous racket of rock was replaced by the sweet-singing voice of a woman, yet singing one of the world's songs. Only one line do I remember. It went something like this, "If there's anybody out there, shine on me."

How fitting it all seemed to be, expressing so eloquently what was etched in the faces of the people as they scurried by, seeking to fill up the present moment. "Is there anybody out there?" "If there is, does He care about me?" "Does He care enough to help me?"

No beggars! No rags! No dirt! But just as lost if they have no Christ as Saviour, no God as Father and no hope forever. Now what will my excuse be? We speak the same language. We live in the same culture. How can I turn from *these* with cold heart and dry eyes and an undisturbed conscience? I am my brother's keeper!

We who have known salvation's day have a Light for their darkness. We have the Bread for their hunger, the Water of life for their burning thirst and the Hope for their emptiness. Whatever will our answer be when we give account at the last?

May God help us not to be ashamed of the Lord Jesus, nor His gospel. As we prostrate ourselves before Him, confessing the sin of loveless hearts, it may be in His mercy He will touch us with the tincture of His love for the lost and open again the floodgates of our tears and unloose these stammering tongues to tell His love, "immense unsearchable."

> *"Shall we, whose souls are lighted with wisdom from on high,*
> *Shall we to men benighted, the lamp of life deny?*
> *Salvation! Oh, salvation! The joyful sound proclaim,*
> *Till earth's remotest station has learned Messiah's Name."*

Balm for the Weary

The Weeping Prophet cried out in his perplexity, "Is there no balm in Gilead?" As we look out on the sorrows of the saints, their burdens and weariness, we too might cry, "Is there no balm?" Is there no relief from the pressures and confusion of life as so many find it?

Let it be emphatically declared: "There IS a balm!" It is a balm that cools the fevered mind and quietens the troubled spirit. Its healing virtue has been enjoyed by many. It clears the vision, strengthens the resolve and comforts the heart. It has nothing to do with cute formulas nor slick slogans. It is God's remedy—sure, suitable and available to every believer. The prescription is readable and may be applied day or night, when at rest or in the midst of much activity. Here it is!

"Consider Him that endured such contradiction of sinners against Himself, lest ye be wearied and faint in your minds" (Heb. 12:3). To bathe the mind with the balm of considering Christ is to know relief from the fever of life and rest from its agitations and fears.

What is this "considering" and how is it practically applied from day to day? The word "consider" is to reckon, to compare, to weigh in the mind. This word is given in Hebrews 12 to a people who had begun well (10:32-34), but when the way became hard and the road uphill, they were tempted to faint and turn back. The Holy Spirit, the Comforter calls upon them to consider the Great Exemplar, not only as an inspiration drawing them on to finish well, but as their Strength and Solace along the way.

To consider Christ is to consider the "what" of Christ. What did He do? He endured the cross and despised the shame for the joy that was set before Him. To bathe the mind with thoughts of the cross will assure us of His great love in times of uncertainty. It will keep us tender and preserve us from the hardening process that the world can have upon us. It will draw us closer to one another, for it is at the cross we most agree. To contemplate the cross is to recall what it cost our Saviour to redeem us and to remember the blood-bought value of every child of God. It will elicit a song again from lips become silent in praise, and tears from eyes that have been dry too long.

> *"Bane and blessing, pain and pleasure,*
> *By the cross are sanctified;*
> *Peace is there that knows no measure,*
> *Joys that through all time abide."*

To consider Christ is to consider the "who" of Christ. Who is He? He is "Jesus," the Saviour! Saviour of the soul from perishing. Saviour of the life from wasting. Saviour of the mind from despairing. He is the Author and Finisher of faith—Source and Sufficiency; Designer and Completer; Vanguard going before and Rereward protecting behind. Consider who He is by the Names He possesses, the titles He bears, and the offices He fills. Consider who He is by the types He fulfills and the emblems He expresses. Consider who He is to the Father, to the Spirit, to the whole flock of God, and to the weakest lamb.

To consider Christ is to consider the "where" of Christ. Where is He now? "Set down at the right hand of the throne of God." What consolation in the dark to know that the darkness and the light are alike to Him. What security in the storm to know that the winds are all in His fist. What peace in a world at war to remember that this One is the Lord of hosts, both of the armies of heaven and of earth. What a balm in grief to remember that He is touched with the feeling of our weaknesses and that He knows what it feels like to suffer. What tranquility to be assured that all power is in His hand, that He does according to the counsel of His own will and none can overrule His authority. What dignity we may have when we remember we are identified with the One who "is gone into heaven, angels and principalities and powers being made subject unto Him"!

To consider Christ is to consider the "why" of Christ. Why did He love me so? Why does He deal with me so? For as we are exercised before God as to the why of our circumstances, we learn that He has a purpose in it all that there might be the peaceable fruit of righteousness in abundance. We may be preoccupied with the rod and be filled with fear. We may be taken up with the pain and be distressed. We may be full of self-pity because of our situation. But by none of these is the purpose of the Lord fulfilled. "Consider Him . . . lest ye be wearied." The contemplation of *who* He is confirms us in our faith. The realization of *what* He is assures us as to our future; we are secure in Him. The contemplation of *where* He is restores our feelings of joy and hope. The wonderment of *why* He loved and came and died for such as we, preserves us from fainting in the way.

The Risk of Rest

She lay heavily in the bed. It had been some years since she was well enough to move around. In spite of the fact that she had left the shores of England a lifetime ago, she had not lost any of her broad accent, nor her north-country sense of humour.

She was quick to remind us, when we visited her, just exactly how many days . . . or weeks had passed since we last had been there. She looked forward to these visits. A week so swiftly rushes by when we are in the whirl of busy lives and daily demands, but an hour can be interminable for those who lie waiting for the knock at the door to signal the coming of a friend.

She loved the pearl of Psalms, so after some conversation, I took out the Book and opened to those familiar words and began to read, "The Lord is my Shepherd; I shall not want. He maketh me to lie down in green pastures . . ." "Stop!" she said, putting out her hand to tap my Bible, "You didn't read that right!" So I began again, certain that it was her hearing and not my reading that was remiss. "The Lord is my Shepherd; I shall not want. He maketh me to lie down . . ." She cut me off short this time, "You're still not reading that right." "What is the mistake I am making?" I asked. "Let me read it for you" she said, "for this is how it must be read: The Lord is my Shepherd; I shall not want. He MAKETH me to lie down . . ." Her broad north country accent stretched out the word and added volume to it. "You see," she said, "most of us silly sheep don't have the sense nor the will to lie down when we should, so the Shepherd sometimes has to MAKE us lie down."

It would be good if some of us would learn those lessons from the lives of others who have gone down the road longer and walked a bit closer to the Shepherd, but it seems we have to feel the rod and staff for ourselves. Our very heartbeat is a constant reminder of the wisdom of God as it pulsates, beat . . . rest, beat . . . rest, beat . . . rest. We are not immortal yet and these bodies, if we are to serve the Lord efficiently, must be given the opportunity to replenish their energies for the long haul.

One esteemed servant of the Lord, who laboured on into his eighties, told me one day, "Some say it is better to burn out than to rust out, but I believe it is best of all to last out, for hopefully we are of more good to God's people as we get older." This is not the sloth of halfhearted effort, forever malingering and planning to do great things next year for God. It is just the wise recognition of the danger signals that say it is time to rest awhile. Not give up to an early "retirement," but just to replenish the diminished physical and spiritual resources. (Somewhere I imagine a reader saying or thinking, "Physician, heal thyself.") True, this is not an easy lesson to learn.

What is the meaning of the title, then, "The Risk of Rest"? If rest is vital, where is the risk? There is a very subtle danger about rest. Perhaps not so much during the rest, but after it. We read the record of God's goodness to Israel in Nehemiah 9, and marvel at His grace and their folly. The pattern seemed to be—blessing, carelessness, disobedience, discipline, and restoration. Time and time again it happened. Then we read in verse 28, "But after they had rest, they did evil again before Thee." That is the risk of rest. Physical relaxation can lead to spiritual relaxation and we can let down our guard long enough for the enemy to make inroads into our mind's attention and our heart's affection.

When we make plans for much needed vacations and for the essential refreshment of the body and the mind and the replenishing of the soul and spirit, let us be aware of the dangers, too. For the enemy ever seeks advantage over us. May we have the sense to lie down in the green pastures before the Shepherd has to MAKE us. May we be aware, too, that the enemy seeks to attack us when we are weary. While we rest our bodies and ease our minds from the pressures of life, let us not relax our vigil lest it also be said of us that "after they had rest, they returned to do evil."

"Then hush! oh, hush! for the Father portioneth as He will,
To all His beloved children, and shall not they be still?
Is not His will the wisest, is not His choice the best?
And in perfect acquiescence is there not perfect rest?

Hush! oh, hush! for the Father, whose ways are true and just,
Knoweth and careth and loveth, and waits for thy perfect trust;
The cup He is slowly filling shall soon be full to the brim,
And infinite compensations forever be found in Him." —F. R. Havergal

Autumn Glory

Bushels of corn, bundles of gladiola, bunches of grapes, and burning leaves all seem to send out a signal to me each year about this time that the summer is ended and the harvest is past. This is not a sad thing for me because there is always something especially beautiful about the autumn in our part of the country. Crimson and gold leaves emblazoned against blue skies delight the viewer and inspire the artist. The only negative thing is that it is so brief. Only a few weeks, then come the rain and wind that tear the leaves from the trees, leaving only stark skeletons to face the winter snows.

Old age is really the autumn of life and should, for the believer in Christ, be radiant and rich in the joy of life and full of the fruit of long fellowship with God. I know a man like that. He just celebrated his 90th birthday. A working man all his life into his 70's, he shepherded the flock of God where he has been for a lifetime. He still rejoices among the saints and is a benediction to his family.

Since "Better is the end of a thing than the beginning thereof," it is clearly important to finish well. Not all do. Some fall by the way and others end in the gall of bitterness, full of self-pity that makes their company and conversation a burden even to those who love them. What, then, is the secret of a happy life and a radiant old-age that blesses the saints like a golden sunset?

That was the question I put to the old veteran. His reply was as uncomplicated as his life. "Satisfaction," he replied, "first with the Lord Jesus Christ. If we are truly satisfied with Him, we will be satisfied with His provision."

I've known this man for over forty years, and can testify that this was no trite piece of religious jargon, but the expression of a life lived according to that principle. I know this because it has been manifested in certain qualities which, it seems to me, should characterize all who belong to the Lord. Here are some of them:

A thankful spirit: "Lots to be thankful for" has been a daily expression for him even when times were tough. Thanklessness breeds discontent and leads to departure from God, as the heathen in Romans 1 discovered to their grief.

A gospel zeal: He has never lost his freshness in the gospel, so that very few ever escape his company without hearing a word of joyful testimony. He has learned what many forget today and indeed deny, that while "the preaching of the cross is to them that perish, foolishness . . . unto us which are saved it is the power of God."

A love for the Word of God: This old believer learned at an early age that there is no substitute for the daily reading of the Word. Now, in old age when studying is really in the past, there is a rich resource of Bible knowledge on which to draw for every circumstance.

A love for the people of God: Some think that when they "retire," then they will get around to visiting and helping the Lord's people and winning a few souls. Well, it doesn't usually happen that way. It is most unlikely that suddenly we will have a care for the flock of God in old age if we have not felt their burdens throughout our lives. Many keep young in heart by caring for others, and even their mental alacrity and physical well-being can know the benefit of sacrificial ministry.

An appreciation of the meaning and privilege of the Lord's Supper: The worshipful spirit will always be full and have some spiritual sustenance to impart. That is a divine principle. When God gets His portion from the life first, then He will respond lavishly with spiritual blessings in heavenly places in Christ.

These qualities, bound together by faith and prayer, have provided for that old soldier of the Cross a happy, fruitful, and contented life. He has lived to see the salvation of his children, all his grandchildren and now his great-grandchildren as they come, one by one, to the years of understanding. Is he rich? I'll say he is! Not in the gold of man's minting, but in the true riches that will withstand the impact of death and the collapse of the universe.

Since these principles have worked so well for him and countless others, should we not follow this example? If we do, we can expect to enjoy what he has found: "At evening time, it shall be light."

> *Eye hath not seen, tongue hath not told, and ear hath not heard it sung,*
> *How buoyant and bold, though it seems to grow old, is the heart, forever young;*
> *Forever young—though life's old age hath every nerve unstrung:*
> *The heart, the heart is a heritage that keeps the old man young!*

Fruitful Days

The equator is watching the sun at its height,
The equinox evens the day and the night;
The springtime is gone with its shoots in the snow,
The summer is signalling soon it must go;
Now 'tis the autumn all blazing with gold,
Declaring the seasons are soon growing old.

The people have watched as we climbed to the height,
The labour demanded the day and the night,
But youth has all gone with its dreams in the skies,
And manhood has blossomed—how quickly it flies!
But now 'tis the autumn of life, we are told,
That this is the season our hands to enfold.

But look at the autumn! Its banners unfurled,
Its crimson and scarlet is flaming our world;
The maple, the aspen, the pine standing high,
All burnished with glory against the blue sky;
The vine clustered heavily perfumes the soil,
The husbandman gathers the fruit of his toil.

If you have been told that your work is all done,
And now it is time just to bask in the sun,
Remember that you have the wisdom of years,
And mingled your griefs and your joys with your tears;
Declare God's great faithfulness, tell forth His praise,
And your autumn can be the most fruitful of days.

The Crisis or the Christ

The Christian life was not intended to be governed by a list of complicated rules and regulations, of actions and corresponding reactions. It was never presented by the Lord Jesus as a system of matter-of-fact answers for the hard facts of life. "The just shall live by faith" (Heb. 10:38, etc.) is a life-transforming principle, broad and deep, applicable to absolutely every realm of the believer's life.

One of the enemy's devices to loosen the tackling of our lives and bring down the mast in hopes of tragic shipwreck, is that of *diversion.* How subtle it is, how smooth and—sad to say—how successful. "Thy tacklings are loosed; they could not well strengthen the mast, they could not spread the sail: then is the prey of a great spoil divided" (Isa. 33:23).

The proliferation of books, tapes and films which focus on Christian conflicts and Christian crisis is inundating the saints. Instead of the considering of Christ, there is a preoccupation with the crisis. We loudly proclaim that the Word of God is the rule of life for us, sacred and sufficient, then clutch at straws (some of them rather expensive!) of "Christian" psychology and crisis ministry. The problem with this crisis-oriented ministry is that it is a leaky vessel. When the next crisis comes, we must find another "How to . . ." book, another "Why this? . . ." film, another "Who me? . . ." tape, or make another pilgrimage to the latest matrimonial mecca, though that may be a thousand or more miles away. There we hope for another diagnosis and hopefully a happier prognosis.

We do not doubt the sincerity of those who offer such books, tapes, and films, and we dare not judge their motives, but perhaps all unwittingly so much of this is a great diversion from the Lord Himself as the All-Sufficient answer.

Chastening, for instance, is the lot of every child of God. But when a crisis comes, we can react in different ways. We may despise it ("I can handle it"). We may "endure" it, and with stiffened backbone and jutted jawbone determine to "tough it out." We may fear the rod and faint altogether. But by none of these is the purpose of chastening fulfilled. We are to be "exercised" by it. That is, we are to take a sensible view of the crisis and recognize that God has planned or permitted it to produce in us the peaceable fruit of righteousness.

How can we be preserved? We may be taken up with the crisis and flee to the latest film on the subject. We may be consumed with the pain of it and give up. Or, hopefully, we may "consider Him that endured such contradiction of sinners against Himself, lest (we) be wearied and faint in (our) minds."

Simple answers are often scorned by the pseudo-intellectual as "simplistic," as though these ignored the complexities and complications of life. Simple answers from God, however, are not necessarily easy answers to apply to the problem. For the complexities that beset a lost sinner, the Lord Jesus says, "Come"—"Call"— "Open"—"Enter," and so on. Simple? Yes! but not *easy.* Such simple responses, you see, involve turning from self and works, to Christ by faith, and that is not easy.

So for the believer in the crisis, it is not turning to this seminar or that system or the other solution. For an *abiding* answer it must be a turning to Christ Himself by faith, the Sufficient One, out of whom flows the fullness of all we need. Then the *purpose* of the crisis will be not lost nor misdirected by the premature application of slick formulas and cute slogans.

Paul had to warn the Galatians, "Are ye so foolish? Having begun in the Spirit, are ye now made perfect by the flesh?" (Gal. 3:3). Sanctification is not by good works any more than salvation is by good works. Good works and right living are the *fruit* of the sanctified life, not the root of it.

If I love the Lord truly with my whole heart, I will love His Word, I will love His people, I will love my spouse, I will love my family, I will love the lost. Simple? Yes, but not easy. There are no formulas, no mental gymnastics, no cute couplets that can produce love. That demands the exercise of faith in turning from all other alternatives, be they ever so wonderful, to the Lord Himself, to be occupied with Him as the Source, the Sufficiency, and the Satisfaction of the soul.

Let us switch off our film projectors and tape recorders, and close those "How to . . ." books for a while; let's get back to the Word of God for ourselves to seek His face and to live by faith. Then we will prove our faith is real by our works. We will be more ready to learn and more easy to live with. Then we can leave the seminars, the slick presentations to the crowds who flock to the broken cisterns, for we will have found the Fountainhead.

# In All the Scriptures

Book of wondrous depths and heights, and glories ever new,
Which in ten thousand various lights brings Jesus into view;
O who would leave the Fountainhead to drink the muddy stream,
Where man has mixed what God hath said with every dreamer's dream?

This, surely, is the beauty of the Word of God, the Bible. It brings the Lord Jesus into view. In every book of the Bible can be seen some aspect or other of His glorious person.

What an experience it must have been for those two saddened disciples on the Emmaus Road so long ago. The Master Expositor drew near to them and opened to them the Scriptures. He expounded "in all the Scriptures" the things concerning Himself. What an exposition! What a "ministry meeting"! What an Expositor! What a Subject!

Later that same night, the Lord confirmed the fact that He was the theme of Old Testament Scriptures. "These are the words which I spake unto you, while I was yet with you, that all things must be fulfilled, which were written in the law of Moses, and in the prophets, and in the psalms, concerning Me" (Lk. 24:44).

The New Testament is yet a fuller revelation of Christ. In the Gospels, the cry is, "Behold, He dies!" In the Acts, the word is, "Behold, He lives!" In the Epistles, it is, "Behold, He comes!" In the Apocalypse, "Behold, He reigns!"

Because of the vastness, indeed the infinity of this glorious subject, every linguistic and descriptive device is brought into play. There are statements in plain language, predicting and describing events concerning the person and work of Christ, His birth, life, sufferings, death, resurrection and glory. There are distinct prophetic types that help us appreciate aspects of this wondrous person. There are types that are happenings such as the Passover. Types that are people—such as David, Melchizedek, Jonah—that teach truths of Christ. There are types that are objects, such as the lamb, the manna, the rock, the serpent on the pole. Symbols and offices, events and institutions pile upon one another to convey facets of beauty, aspects of character, person and purposes, wonders and workings, sufferings and glories of our beloved Lord Jesus Christ.

Every realm is harvested for illustrations, if by some means the glories and wonders of Christ may be made known to the sons of men. From the heavens—the sun, the morning star, the light—all beam forth glories in the Word that speak of Him. From the atmosphere—the dew, the sparrow, the pelican, the owl, the turtle dove—tell something of Him. From the earth—the lily, the tender plant, the root, the stem, the branch, the vine. Waters above and waters beneath bespeak His refreshing fullness. The stones of architecture and the seeds of agriculture are used to tell forth His glories, too. The weapons of the armory—sword and shield and buckler—are called to portray aspects of His infinite being in the conflict of the ages.

Colours of pigment and tones of music, flashings of lightning and noises of thunder are added to the panoply of descriptions, if by these the senses might apprehend more of His fullness and perfections from the Word of God.

So we go on, higher and broader, longer and deeper into the Word, only to find that the more we have discovered of the Lord in the Word, the more we find that there are yet infinities stretching out before us beyond the limits of spiritual vision as we possess it now, and on into the vanishing point of the mind and over the horizons of eternity. At last, as we behold His glories in the Word, His revealed excellencies and beauties, we feel like the bride in the Song, as we stand amazed in His presence: "Yea, He is . . . He really is . . . altogether lovely."

Turn your eyes upon Jesus,
Look full in His wonderful face,
And the things of earth
Will grow strangely dim,
In the light of His glory and grace.
                    —H. H. Lemmel

Review and Preview

We cannot help but be amazed at the seemingly ever increasing speed of passing time. As we look backwards over the years of our past, there is always a strange co-mingling of emotion. There is the backward look of sacred recollection, the good, the happy, the holy memories that even now bring something of the glow of God upon us. David knew this when in Psalm 63 his longing was mixed with hope as he remembered when God had drawn near in the sanctuary. The writer to the Hebrews exhorted them to "call to remembrance the former days" of early faith and endurance in affliction. Yes, there are memories that waft across the mind like the summer breeze, stirring the fragrance of life and warming the soul.

There are the other memories, of course. Like the backward look of sad remorse. These rise up unbidden and chill the soul. Failure and sin, actions taken we cannot eradicate, words spoken we would give almost anything if we could silence their haunting echo. Yet such debilitating recollections do us harm. If all has been done before God that is possible by confession and restitution, we must put them under the blood and leave them there.

This is what Paul meant, I believe, when he wrote to the saints at Philippi, "Forgetting those things which are behind" (3:13). That is, things the memory of which will only spoil and weaken us for God. By choice and by will, we are to refuse to ponder on such. What things did Paul refer to? *The things that should have been*, associated with the failures of others. He speaks of "your lack of service toward me" (2:30). Regaling the mind with the failures of the saints towards us in the past is a pathetic occupation. The Israelites never ate of the "sinew that shrank" for that would only remind them of Jacob's failure. Sad to say, it is not unknown for believers to feed themselves (and one another) with this scrawny fare, duly garnished with bitter herbs. Paul says, "Forget it."

The things that might have been likewise can distress the mind and rob us of present joy. Paul's flawless reputation as an Israelite and what he might have been in the nation, had it not been for the Damascus road encounter, he only counted as loss (3:5-7). Someone wrote, "Of all the words by lip or pen, the saddest are: what might have been." Such frustrated recollections can only drag upon the soul. Paul says, "Forget it."

The things that cannot be often assail the mind. It takes maturity to accept the inevitable. If we don't, we will exhaust our energies beating on doors that God in His wisdom and mercy has closed to us. What relief to fall into the embrace of the perfect will of God. To continually recall those things that cannot now be, is a draining exercise in futility. Paul says, "Forget it." He had made a grand choice, and so there were things that never could be as a result.

There is also the forward look. To some timorous souls, there is a fear about the future because it is in the realm of the unknown. To others who are visionaries, the future is one great dream boat full of good intentions. Paul has a sensible view of the past and of the future. He saw there were things behind him to forget, but there were things before him to be inspired by. Always first it was the Lord. "We look for the Saviour" (3:20). For Paul, his inspiring hope was a sight of the Saviour. His aging body, in which he suffered for his beloved Master, would then be transformed, "Who shall change our vile body." So another inspiration was a change of the body. But Paul had long vision, and he saw onwards to the great day of conquest and the Lord's power to "subdue all things." So as this great servant moved through the world, he viewed it all in the light of the subjection of all things to Christ. But Paul's sensible view of the past and his inspiring view of the future did not rob him of his sense of responsibility in the present: "This one thing I do . . . I press toward the mark" (3:13-14). Daily he stretched himself out for the prize.

As the year fades into the mists of the past, and we look as well as we can into the days ahead, let us be wise, rejoicing in the recollections of God's faithfulness with us, whether in delights or in disciplines. As much as in us is, and with the Lord's help, refuse to ponder on those things, the memory of which will only weaken. Then with a hopeful outlook for the future to inspire us, may we buckle down to do the one thing we can do today—press on.

Faint not, Christian, though the road leading to thy blest abode
Darksome be and dangerous, too; Christ, thy Guide, will bring thee through.
Faint not, Christian, Christ is near; soon in glory He'll appear;
Then shall end thy toil and strife, death be swallowed up of life.

A Followers

package of photographs came back from the developers the other day. They were mostly taken over the year-end holidays, when the family were all gathered together. As we looked over the snapshots, it was a happy few moments as we smiled and laughed at one and another of the pictures. Some were posed, some caught unawares, some quite photogenic, then others of us not quite so. But there was one that had been in the camera since the summer, and was just now printed with the recent shots. As I looked at it, suddenly there was a flashback from years ago. In my memory I could feel the chubby hand of a little fellow and hear again his boyish voice.

The photo before me showed my younger son pushing the lawn mower across the grass on a lovely summer day. Behind him about two or three paces, his own little fellow, walking in his footsteps, pensively watching his dad's feet. What flashed back to my mind was an incident that made me seriously think about the course of my own life.

My son, Bill, was just a little fellow then, about 3 or 4 years of age. We were out walking, just the two of us together, on one of those golden days of summer. There is always something special about those quality times with the little children. I don't remember the subject of our conversation, but I will not easily forget what happened. We walked on, often in silence, for Bill never rattled on, but would think a bit, and then speak. I enjoyed the quietness and the feel of his little hand in mine. I knew he was thinking, and something was coming. "Daddy," he said, looking up.

"Yes, son," I waited.

"Daddy, wherever you go, I'm going to go."

It hit me like a bolt. "Wherever you go, I'm going to go"! Ever since the children had been born, we had prayed that they would be saved in their childhood and that their hands would be clean and their feet would be led in the paths of righteousness. But those words from my little son made me realize just what a responsibility I had as a father, to contribute to the answer of my own prayers. The power of example has more influence on our children than the eloquence of our sermons. Our children learn more of God, the reality of the Christian life, and of eternal values, as they watch and listen to us in the home, day by day.

How we act, and how we react in the circumstances of life, will be a greater sermon than anything they will ever hear from the platform. Their convictions as to the reality of the Christian life, and of a God who hears and answers prayer, are being formed as they see it displayed before their eyes at home sweet home.

Abraham is identified with tents and altars. He "pitched his tent . . . he builded an altar" (Gen. 12:8). The first thing his children saw as they stepped out of the tent in the morning was the altar. By pitching his tent, he witnessed he was a stranger passing through. By building his altar, he witnessed that he was a worshipper of God. It is not surprising, then, to read the commendation of the Lord in Genesis 18:19, "I know him, that he will command his children and his household after him, and they shall keep the way of the Lord."

Isaac is identified with the digging of wells. Of this son of Abraham, we read, "He builded an altar . . . and pitched his tent there; and there Isaac's servants digged a well" (Gen. 26:25). "Like father, like son," we say. How wonderful when we can give our children the example of a pilgrim character, and provide the family altar for them before they go out every day to face the world. We may give them the added benefit of a joyful home where laughter is no stranger, for joy is the bucket with which we "draw water out of the wells of salvation" (Isa. 12:3). We do our children the most profound disservice if we send them out to the influence of a humanistic school system without first letting them hear us surround them with prayer. It is sad to think that some children may go out to school without proper food to nourish their brains and their bodies, but sadder still for Christian parents to send them out without the assurance that they have been prayed for and that God profoundly cares for them personally.

Those words still echo in my memory, "Daddy, wherever you go, I'm going to go." We can only hope and pray that our children and their children will be preserved from the by-paths, sidetracks, stony ground, and dead ends where some of us have gone. God has been merciful to us, and we who are parents can keep praying that wherever we go, and our children follow, we will ever lead them to the Lord Jesus and into the ways of holiness and peace.

Elbows and Eyelids

The love of God for His creature is made evident in ten thousand ways. It is the sheer bounty of it, the overflowing abundance of it, the incredible munificence of His lavish love that staggers the mind to explore, and impoverishes human language to express.

Before the first man ever inhaled his first enlivening breath, the breath of God Himself, before he ever opened his eyes on that fair Paradise and scanned the radiant spectrum of undiminished light on the verdant hills, the Creator already had designed such a provision for man's joy and satisfaction that God Himself could say by the Divine measure that it was all "good."

Everywhere in nature we see this extravagance of God's love and wisdom. The encyclopedia records that there are over 4,700 different species of grass! There are more than 90,000 varieties of butterflies! There are over 200,000 varieties of beetles!

The Psalmist lifted his eyes above this magnificent profusion to the heavens and marvelled at the starry worlds that dusted the vaults of space with spangled glory. Viewing this vast realm of celestial wonder he exclaimed, "What is man, that Thou art mindful of him?" (Ps. 8:3-4).

David, considered the wonder of his own frame and wrote, "I am fearfully and wonderfully made" (Ps. 139:14). Many of us in good health take for granted this marvellous design. We likely never give thanks to God for His love shown in such ordinary things as elbows and eyelids.

What if we had no eyelids! To sleep we would have to roll our eyes up to shut out the light. What about elbows? If we had just one long bone from shoulder to wrist, just think how we would be incapacitated for even the simplest tasks, like feeding ourselves. Consider the marvels of the human hand. The surgeon can knot a suture finer than a human hair with two fingers inside an ailing heart. The builder picks up a concrete block with his hand and puts it in place. God did not put all this sophisticated control and gripping, lifting power in the hand, but in the brain and arms; otherwise our hands would be clumsy masses of brain tissue and muscle.

Doctors could explain to us much more of the vast network of nerves, the complicated balance of chemicals, blood, and electrical impulses that continually carry, sustain and control our life functions, moment by moment. Most of the time we are oblivious to this continual, unobtrusive flood of the beneficence of God. Jeremiah reminds us, "It is of the Lord's mercies that we are not consumed, because His compassions fail not. They are new every morning: great is Thy faithfulness."

Those evidences of God's love in the creature are but a shadow of the riches of His goodness to us all in the highest blessings. The greatest of these is the gift of His own beloved Son. It cannot be better said by man than He has written in that golden text, John 3:16, "For God so loved the world, that He gave His only begotten Son, that whosoever believeth in Him should not perish, but have everlasting life." How sad that there are millions who soak up the daily beneficence of God, yet spurn His love, despise His grace, and reject His beloved Son as Lord and Saviour.

From this Supreme Gift flows all the others: the gift of His Spirit to all who believe and the treasures of His holy Word; the eternal inheritance that the moth cannot eat, the rust cannot rot and the thief cannot steal; the fellowship of saints who, in spite of warts and wrinkles, are still the beautiful people, the salt of the earth, the beloved of God. May it never be written in Heaven's record that those of us who daily bask in the sunshine of such wondrous love are guilty of the ingratitude of those heathen of whom it is written, "Neither were thankful" (Rom. 1:21).

Well, maybe we don't think much about elbows and eyelids, beetles or butterflies, but let us not be unmindful of all God's goodness and what our response ought to be, for "the goodness of God leadeth thee to repentance."

O Lord, from my heart I do thank Thee for all Thou has borne in my room,
Thine agony, dying unsolaced, alone in the darkness of doom,
That I, in the glory of heaven, forever and ever might be—
A thousand, a thousand thanksgivings, I bring, blessed Saviour, to Thee!
　　　　　　　—Ernst C. Homburg *(trans. from the German by Mrs. Frances Bevan)*

Storms

Storms at sea are never pleasant. Awesome, frightening, but hardly enjoyable. Yet the lessons learned in the storm can be of significant value for another day and another circumstance. Almost the whole chapter of Acts 27 is devoted to the events surrounding a storm. There are lessons we may learn from this storm. God knows that each of us at some time or other must pass through our own deep waters. It is not "If thou passest through the waters," it is "When . . . "

One lesson is that *God allows His people to suffer alongside the ungodly in the circumstances of life.* God's servants were in that storm because the sailors would not believe the words of Paul. Many of the Lord's people must suffer because of the attitude of those who will not believe. Salvation of the soul is no escape from the common trials of life . . . not yet. The fallacy of the false gospel that declares, "God wants you healthy and God wants you wealthy" has driven many a simple soul into despair when they suffer pain and poverty. If it was preached instead, "God wants you holy," that would be in harmony with the Word.

Another lesson we may learn is that *Christians in the same circumstance may have quite different reactions.* Luke writes, No sun . . . no stars . . . no small tempest . . . no hope (v. 20). He was consumed with the power of the storm and what he seemed to have lost. Was the sun extinguished? Were the stars switched off? Above the storm they shone as ever in their place. What about Paul? He was up on deck, shouting above the gale, "Cheer up . . . all is well." In the same storm one was downcast while the other was delighting in the promise of God and cheering others.

God often blesses unbelievers because of the presence of His people. God was not only going to save faithful Paul, but also fearful Luke. More than this, He was going to save the faithless sailors. This was for the sake of His servants on that ship (v. 24). How little at times do unbelievers realize what they owe to the Lord's people among them. Their preservation, their provision, perhaps their very paycheck is the result of the prayers and the presence of some unappreciated believer in their midst.

In the storms of life, *God shows through His people who is really in control.* Paul was only one of about 250 prisoners on board. But when the circumstance reached crisis proportions and the sailors and master of the ship were at a loss to know what to do next, it is Paul who steps forward and on the basis of God's sovereign control brings some hope and order to things.

How good to be assured in every circumstance that it is "Jesus Christ: who is gone into heaven, and is on the right hand of God; angels and authorities and powers being made subject unto Him" (1 Pet. 3:21-22). Things may get out of our control, but nothing *ever* gets out of His control.

When things are at their darkest, the Christian still has hope and *God uses His people to present the hope to the perishing.* Apart from the promise of God, there is no hope. Apart from the saving message from God, it must only be darkness and despair .

What a lesson for us in this day of drift and confusion. The sailors did not want to hear some cute anecdote, some eloquent, honeyed sermon, some cold analysis of Scripture. They would have despaired if all Paul had to offer was some new "method" of doing things. What they needed and what they got from the servant of God was the only thing that mattered—a message from God.

Lost sinners today can be "excited" by light and frivolous methods. They can be amused by interesting anecdotes. They can be impressed by eloquent dissertations. They can be influenced to give money, time, and effort. But by none of these is the urgent need of their souls met. They need a word from God in the power of the Holy Spirit.

Then let us "Preach the Word . . . for the time will come when they will not endure sound doctrine; but after their own lusts shall they heap to themselves teachers, having itching ears; and they shall turn away their ears from the truth, and shall be turned unto fables" (2 Tim. 4:2-4).

Storms today may sweep us,
But the Lord will keep us
We shall have His presence ever nigh;
He is here beside us
To uphold and guide us—
Endless joy is coming by and by.

Think Not . . .

(Psalm 12:5)
Think not thou canst sigh
In silence of the night,
Or yet in all the clamour of the day,
And not be heard by Him,
Who is ever nigh.

(2 Kings 20:5)
Think not there can flow,
Unnoticed from thine eye,
One single tear of sorrow or of pain,
And is not seen by Him
Who loves you so.

(Psalm 107:9)
Think not in thy heart,
Concealed from human eye,
The deepest untold longing, aching there,
And is not known by Him
Who can impart.

(Psalm 34:4)
Think not there's a fear,
Betimes that chills the breast,
Untold to even those we dearly love,
And is not sensed by Him
Whose power is near.

(1 John 1:9)
Think not there's a sin
So secret in the heart,
Confessed, tho' none but He should know,
And is not cleansed by Him
Whose life's within.

(Psalm 37:4)
Think not thy request
Poured out in solitude,
Lest others hearing, should not understand,
Is never heard by Him,
Who grants the best.

(Isaiah 58:10-11)
Think not thou shalt dwell
Always in the shade,
As surely as the dawn, thy sun shall shine
And thou rejoice through Him
Who doth all well.

(Psalm 30:5)
Ah, then! In thy distress,
Be not thou overwhelmed;
For though, today, thou canst not understand,
It is all known to Him,
*And He **shall** bless.*

God is Faithful

It is said to be a mark of advancing years when we begin to recall more frequently the sights and sounds and scenes of the distant past (and forget where we laid our glasses a moment ago!) If that be so, then I must be getting older because I find myself doing just that.

I can smell them now! Summer days and the tarred ropes coiled in the fishing boat. The sound of the knife blade, rounded by use, cracking open the mussels, deftly scooping them out of the shell and plopping their soft pink-orange flesh into the bait pail. The salt water lapping at the boats, hauled out of the water, and heeled over on the pebble shore. The tangy smell of the seaweed and the cry of the gulls as they swooped and wheeled around our heads looking for a morsel. Then, when we had filled the pail with bait, we got to take one of the dories and row it out beyond the harbour wall and, with a couple of lines, try our skill. Many a fresh, flopping herring we unhooked into the little boat.

Proudly we took them home for mother to roll in oatmeal and fry in butter while we deeply inhaled the aroma. We warmed our fingers at the fire, then with mouth-watering anticipation, sat down to a banquet of oatmeal herring and crusty bread. Ah! Those were the days . . . Were they?

The country was just emerging from deep economic depression. I still recall seeing the long lines of the unemployed. We heard the rumblings of distant wars and little dreamed that so soon we would add to our store of memories the acrid smell of gunpowder, the mournful wail of sirens, terror in the night, the devastation without mercy, death without reason, and young men without a future.

Yet even those troubled and dangerous years yield so many happy memories. Could we ever forget those divine interventions, the fresh discoveries of God in far-off places with strange-sounding names? Or lose the joy of deep friendships formed in the midst of dangers, friendships that have weathered the years till now?

So it is not really the outward things at all, whether marked by the quiet lapping of the waters or the thunderings of war. It is the goodness and faithfulness of God, no matter what the circumstance. We may not always have recognized it, but like an unshakable foundation, there it stands: "The Lord is good" and "God is faithful."

So it is the obligation of all God's people to make known the faithfulness of God to each successive generation that they, in their day of trial or of triumph, may rise up to bless the Lord and learn the song of Ethan the Ezrahite, "I will sing of the mercies of the Lord forever" (Ps. 89:1).

Today will be the yesterday we remember tomorrow. How important that we bless our children with an inheritance of memories rich in eternal values by declaring in our lives and from our lips that the God in whom we have placed our trust can be utterly depended upon in sunshine and in storm, in days of bright prospect and in days of baffling problems. When all around gives way, the Lord will not suffer His faithfulness to fail (Ps. 89:33).

> *Great is Thy faithfulness, O God my Father,*
> *There is no shadow of turning with Thee;*
> *Thou changest not, Thy compassions they fail not;*
> *As Thou hast been Thou forever will be.*
>
> *Summer and winter and springtime and harvest,*
> *Sun, moon, and stars in their courses above,*
> *Join with all nature in manifold witness*
> *To Thy great faithfulness, mercy and love.*
>
> *Pardon for sin and a peace that endureth,*
> *Thine own dear presence to cheer and to guide;*
> *Strength for today and bright hope for tomorrow,*
> *Blessings all mine, with ten thousand beside!*
>
> —T. O. Chisholm

 Pain!

What is this mysterious thing, this universal sorrow, and why? Multitudes throughout the earth today cry out with Jeremiah, "Why is my pain perpetual, and my wound incurable?" Breaking out as a consequence of sin in Eden, it came first to the human race when Eve was promised the sorrowful pangs of childbirth.

Because of sin, things go wrong, but God is merciful to warn us of impending dangers. The leper's problem is that there is a loss of all sensation in the extremities. No pain is felt there and infections destroy those members. So pain is part of the alarm system that warns us something is out of order so steps can be taken.

For the believer, the closer we seek to follow the Master, the more we are led into deeper meanings of the cross. The Lord asked a very solemn question of James and John: "Are ye able to drink of the cup that I shall drink of, and to be baptized with the baptism that I am baptized with?" Their response was, as one, "We are able." The Lord's solemn reply was, "Ye shall drink indeed of My cup, and be baptized with the baptism that I am baptized with" (Mt. 20:20-23). Not that they would share in His expiatory sufferings. Those He must bear alone. But they would taste of that cup, and enter the waters where He would plunge to the very bottom under all the waves and billows of God's judgment against our sins. So pain may be the result of the Lord's dealings with us, that we might learn something, at least by contrast, of His own deep sufferings and wondrous love.

Those who know something of the shuddering pain that racks the whole body and assails the mind to unhinge it, may well ask if there is anyone, even the most loved, for whom they would willingly offer to enter that realm of anguish, in the full knowledge of all it would entail of desperate hours and seemingly endless nights of distress. Perhaps that is why mother-love stands unique among the loves of human hearts.

But there was One who was willing, blessed be His lovely Name! From eternal ages He loved us. Knowing us through and through as poor sinners, He left the comforts of His heavenly home, the holy cry of seraphim, the constant service of angels, and the glory of His throne to suffer and to die. It was in the full and unshielded knowledge of all that He would suffer, He set His face to go to Jerusalem (Lk. 9:51; 18:31-33).

What kind of a love is this? When we think of who He is, the Inhabiter of eternity, God's beloved Son. And when we think of this poor planet, stained with blood, spoiled by sin, inhabited by rebels unworthy even to look up to the vault of heaven, far less go and live there. Yet He loved us notwithstanding all, and came to suffer and die for us. It was not to suffer one mortal agony. He could cry through the psalmist, "The pains of hell gat hold upon Me" (Ps. 116:3).

But there was something far beyond the pains of the beating and the smiting, beyond the agony of the thorn and the nail, beyond the burnings of thirst and of insult. When all that was endured, God drew the mourning-cloth of darkness around His Son, not to protect Him, but that no one should behold except the sorrowing God, the utter depths, the abandoned woes of the Lamb of God as He bore away the sin of the world.

Many have been the sufferers of this weeping race, disfigured and twisted by their pains, but only of God's Perfect Servant, that Man of Sorrows, is it recorded, "His visage was so marred more than any man, and His form more than the sons of men." No man ever saw that visage so marred, nor ever beheld that tormented form, as out yonder in the "land not inhabited," the lovely, lonely Son of God became the scapegoat to bear away the world's sin. All the pangs of hell were gathered together, all the pains of God's judgment found their target in the sinless Sufferer, who "bare our sins in His own body on the tree."

Whatever pain of this life we may have known, even in its extremity, it only leaves us standing amazed and speechless on the shores of a fathomless ocean of the love of God in Christ Jesus, to wonder, to worship, and adore.

For me Thou hast borne the reproaches,
The mockery, hate, and disdain;
The blows and the spittings of sinners,
The scourging, the shame and the pain;
To save me from bondage and judgment,
Thou gladly hast suffered for me,
A thousand, a thousand thanksgivings,
I bring, blessed Saviour, to Thee!
—Ernst C. Homburg *(trans. from the German by Mrs. Frances Bevan)*

"Close Enough?

"Close enough" are words I would not want to hear from a heart surgeon when I'm coming out of the anesthesia, nor from the pilot of the aircraft in which I am flying as he descends through cloud for an instrument landing. Why, then, we must ask, is "close enough" acceptable to so many these days when it comes to obedience in the things of God? Is "close enough" good enough for God?

Carnal alternatives are bad enough, but it is the subtle, pious ones that claim the Word of God for their authority that are so dangerous. They deceive the innocent, divert the elders, distress and confuse the body of believers, and, sad to say, divide the assemblies of the saints.

"Close enough" wasn't good enough on the lake when the Lord told Peter to let down the nets. Peter responded, "Nevertheless *at Thy word* I will let down the net" (Lk. 5:5). That was *not* the word of the Lord. It was close, but the Lord had said "nets." Peter said "net." He modified the word of the Lord to satisfy his own reasoning and fit his own faith. The net broke and he suffered loss.

King Saul was told to pay strict attention to "the voice of the words of the Lord," and utterly destroy Amalek and all that they had. But he spared the king and "the best of the sheep, and the oxen." When challenged by Samuel, Saul replied, "Blessed be thou of the Lord." Sounds so spiritual, doesn't it? The only problem was the background accompaniment, "the bleating of the sheep and the lowing of the oxen." His explanation to God's servant was subtle; he had "spared the best of the sheep and of the oxen, to sacrifice unto the Lord thy God." Close enough wasn't good enough for God that day either, and Saul suffered the loss of the kingdom. He went away with these words ringing in his ears, "Behold, to obey is better than sacrifice."

We could go on to consider other sad cases of close-enough obedience and the sorrowful consequences. When will we learn that hollow hallelujahs, heavenly sweet-talk, and mistaken zeal make a very thin smokescreen indeed? The spiritual eye discerns the true nature of those self-serving programs, the personal empire building, the impressive titles, and claims of religious successes being presented to God's people for support— all claiming, of course, to be authorized by the Word of the Lord.

Surely it was a good thing to let down the net. Surely it is thoroughly biblical to sacrifice unto the Lord. Both Peter and Saul and many of us also have discovered to our sorrow that it is possible to do a good thing in the wrong way, at the wrong time, and for the wrong reasons, and piously claim the authority of Scripture or the example of "early brethren."

What shall we say of great Moses, "mighty in words and deeds." Told to speak to the rock for water, he smote it in anger. Close enough? "Well," one may say, "it was successful; it worked, didn't it? The people got the water." Yes, but that only fulfilled God's promise to supply for His own. Herein lies a great principle often forgotten. *God's blessing on a man or a work is not necessarily a sign of His approval. It is only the vindication of His own Word. God will always honour His Word by whomever and however it is applied, but the servant will always be answerable for the means and methods used.* Moses suffered a grievous, lifelong loss as a result of his action.

In these days, there are programs being offered and methods being taught to catch men in the gospel net. There are constant appeals for sacrifice "unto the Lord" and well-organized movements to "renew" and "revive" God's people. We dare not judge the motives or the men involved, but we can test it all with the plumbline of the Word. Are they, and we, following the New Testament pattern explicitly or just "close enough"? Close enough isn't good enough for God.

Then may Thy perfect, glorious will be evermore fulfilled in me,
And make my life an answering chord of glad, responsive harmony.

Oh! It is life indeed to live within this kingdom strangely sweet;
And yet we fear to enter in, and linger with unwilling feet.

We fear this wondrous will of Thine because we have not reached Thy heart;
Not venturing our all on Thee, we may not know how good Thou art. —Jean Sophia Pigott

---

Editor's note: The distinction is made between the plural noun, *diktua,* nets, and Peter's singular word, *dikton,* one net (see KJV, JND, Bullinger's *Companion Bible,* Newberry, etc.). Some texts and some newer translations, however, do not make the distinction.

Who Blew the Trumpet?

Everyone who has had the experience of being awakened by reveille has at some time, more than likely, thought how much more pleasant it would have been to be gently stirred by the sweet strains of a violin instead of the blistering notes of the bugle. However, there is no doubt that it does get one's attention!

Attention-getters! We find them in every place. They have something within that makes them want to be noticed, to be credited, praised, acknowledged. They crave the podium, the chairman's seat, the place at the head, the public notice. They find it most difficult to play second fiddle. If you want them to participate, then they prefer first trumpet.

King Saul was a trumpet-blower. His son, Jonathan, had won a notable victory over the Philistines at the hill of Geba. The news spread quickly to the rest of the Philistine garrison and eventually back to Saul, well behind the lines of battle. Israel had not yet heard the news report, so, true to form, Saul wanted to be the Announcer. So we read in 1 Samuel 13:3-4, "Jonathan smote the garrison . . . and Saul blew the trumpet . . . and all Israel heard say that *Saul* had smitten a garrison of the Philistines."

Did it matter to Jonathan who got the credit? Seemingly not, as far as the record shows. Shortly after, Jonathan and his armour bearer were off on another sortie while his father relaxed under a pomegranate tree in safety with six hundred men (14:1-2). It only mattered to Jonathan that the work was done and that he should faithfully discharge his duty. Thus he gives evidence of a mature and generous character. Saul, on the other hand, exposes his little soul as he blows his own trumpet and takes the credit for a battle he didn't fight and a victory he didn't personally win.

James reminds us there will always be the "walkers" and there will always be the "talkers." The Lord warns us of the danger of Pharisaism, the desire to be noticed in the public display of religious service. Their motive was "that they may be seen of men."

Of course, it is not wrong in itself to be seen of men; the Lord was seen by thousands. The wrong is when we "love" it. There are many godly servants of Christ who, by the very nature of their work and calling, must be in the public eye, but not to "desire the preeminence."

How beautiful to see the Jonathans doing the work, fighting the battles, ministering to their heavenly David for love of Him and seeking no place nor praise from men. They are happy to take second place and count it an honour. Jonathan, the man in line for the throne of Israel, said to David the shepherd, who was very much in disfavour with King Saul, "Thou shalt be king over Israel, and I shall be next to thee" (1 Sam. 23:17).

In our day, the only message such self-effacing servants trumpet—and they do it with no uncertain sound—is the gospel. They call attention, not to themselves nor to their particular group of followers, but to their Master. The language of their hearts is never "Suffer me first," but in the echo of that most noble soldier, "Not I, but Christ."

If you cannot on the ocean sail among the swiftest fleet,
Rocking on the highest billows, laughing at the storms you meet,
You can stand among the sailors anchored yet within the bay;
You can lend a hand to help them as they launch their boats away.

If you are too weak to journey up the mountain steep and high,
You can stand within the valley while the multitudes go by;
You can chant in happy measure as they slowly pass along,
Though they may forget the singer, they will not forget the song.

Do not then stand idly waiting for some greater work to do;
Fortune is a lazy goddess, she will never come to you;
Go, and toil in any vineyard, do not fear to do or dare;
If you want a field or labour, you can find it anywhere.
—Ellen H. Cotes

Thee or Me?

Psalm 42:1

What do I really desire
In this life?
Is it something for me,
And a little for Thee?
To what do I grandly aspire
In the strife?
Is it THEE, my God, is it THEE?

What drives me onward to serve
Day by day?
Is it something for me,
Or glory for Thee?
What motive enlivens each nerve
In the fray?
Is it THEE, my God, is it THEE?

What is it draws my first love
To impart?
Is it something for me,
Or THEE, only THEE?
What is it, below or above
Fills my heart?
Is it THEE, my God, is it THEE?

Help me to more understand
By Thy grace,
That the best thing for me,
Is enjoyment of THEE;
That blessings and service, though grand
In their place,
Are not THEE, blessed God, are not THEE.

The Lost Art

With the rapid growth of technology in our day, the ever increasing tempo of life and its demands for "sudden service," "speedy mufflers," "in-by-nine-out-by-five," there is a tendency to feel that stillness, quietness, and absence of activity are somehow a waste.

Many ancient arts have been lost altogether. Even crafts of the last generation are being swallowed up by computered monsters. While visiting a farm some time ago where there were two thousand sheep, I was taken to the fold where the lambs were being born. Twelve hundred lambs bleated for attention. But there was a great problem. It was hard to find experienced shepherds. It is becoming one of the lost arts in our technological society.

There is another art that seems to be in great danger. The art of *meditation*. For a child of God, it is not only beneficial but needful for healthy, spiritual life and growth. What is meditation? Primarily it is contemplation. It is the exercise of the mind in viewing thoughts from different angles. Spiritually, of course, in the Christian life it is the contemplation of the Holy Scriptures and of the spiritual thoughts.

In the Old Testament, the two main words that are translated "meditate" carry the idea of "murmuring" or "speaking" to one's self in the mind, to "ponder." In the New Testament, the word "meditate" occurs only once specifically in the Authorized Version, 1 Timothy 4:15. It is translated variously in other versions as being diligent, being wholly occupied, giving care and attention, practicing, and to take pains with certain things.

An examination of these ideas shows that meditation is not simply a matter of letting the mind wander aimlessly into realms of biblical subjects. Rather it is an active directing of the mind to engage itself in controlled and orderly contemplation.

When the Lord said to Joshua in Joshua 1:8: "This book of the law shall not depart out of thy mouth, but thou shalt meditate therein day and night, that thou mayest observe to do according to all that is written therein: for then thou shalt make thy way prosperous, and then thou shalt have good success," He gave him the key to a happy, fulfilled life.

Satan is after the minds of God's people today. He seeks to defile them, to distress them, to distract them, and to divert them from God and the ways of God, to disturb them and if possible to destroy them. The fierce pressures today, on the minds of believers, rob them of peace and oftentimes the ability to concentrate on the study of the Scriptures. Even to pray for more than a few minutes sometimes becomes a difficulty.

Meditation, the lost art, is like a balm to the weary mind. It is to hear the Lord speak peace to the storm within, or to raise the believer above the storm and to see it all from God's point of view.

The world is coming to see the great value of "meditation." So we have the great popularity of meditative cults all promising life in a new dimension. But spiritual, healthful, biblical meditation is not day-dreaming, letting the mind run free even into biblical thoughts. We can see from the words used, it is to have an Object. The Written Word and the Living Word are the only permissible obsessions for the believer. The will is to direct the thoughts, "bringing into captivity every thought to the obedience of Christ" (2 Cor. 10:5).

The gracious Spirit of God will readily assist the willing mind in this holy, joyous occupation and lead the thoughts into fields of new discovery and sweet recollections. It is to engage in spiritual explorations into the infinities of God, secrets that are only given to those who are willing to spend the time in this seeming inactivity, which some feel to be a "waste of precious time."

So meditation is speaking to one's self in the language and thoughts of Scripture. It is pondering, turning thoughts over to view them from this aspect and from that. It is a diligent occupation of the mind with scriptural words and thoughts with a view of not only discovering but of expressing what is discovered, by word or deed to others.

This is what sustains the mind in times of stress, refreshes it in times of weariness, comforts it in times of sorrow. For thinking with God is a veritable balm to the mind. The servant of the Lord will, by this, keep fresh and interesting in his ministry and will always have something to impart to the people of God. It soon becomes evident when a man has spent time in meditation.

A Call to the Shepherds

Crises in the Middle East, growing tensions in Europe, violence in Britain, the stirrings of power in the Far East, all give the media ample cause for dramatic headlines and special newscasts. But there is a crisis of the most serious kind having tragic consequences and of even greater significance than the trouble of the nations, yet it never hits the headlines. It is the subtle, methodical and merciless attack on the Church by the sworn enemy of God and His people, the devil.

The wiles of this formidable enemy are masterful. He seldom opens his attack with a barrage from without. He knows that this would only draw the saints together in defense. Rather, it is by insidious infiltration he first seeks to weaken the structure and to cause confusion among those charged with the care of the flock of God.

It has become apparent to any intelligent viewer that there is a definite strategy, a methodical and cunningly devised conspiracy aimed at destroying the collective and personal testimony of the saints.

The shepherds know what to do with a slavering wolf coming from the outside, tearing at the flock. A wolf in sheep's clothing, however, rising up in the midst is quite another thing.

The overall strategy seems to be to confuse and divide the leadership first. Once that is accomplished, that confusion will spread like a poison through the assembly. We see examples of this in both Old and New Testaments. In Judges 5:8, there was "war in the gates." That is not war with an enemy. That is fighting among the leaders themselves. Confusion falls upon the people. They walk in the "crooked ways" instead of the highway (v. 6). That is confusion of purpose. They turn from the living God to No-gods. That is confusion of allegiance. They are bereft of both the means of defense and attack, having neither shield nor spear. That is confusion of weaponry.

Where there is a clear-thinking loyalty to God and to the unchallenged authority of His Word, the people of God will know a strength and a security in times of attack. Where there is weakness and disunity among the leaders and a hesitancy to deal with uncomfortable issues, there will be confusion and distress among the people.

The time is come when the shepherds must truly lead the flock of God, by spiritual example and by exhibiting those qualities of spiritual courage that will expose the insidious infiltration of evil, even though it be robed in duplicity and spouting pious platitudes to deceive the simple and to gather a following to itself.

We are creatures of extremes and the enemy knows this. His strategy then is to impose either a legalism that demands an outward conformity to man-made rules at the expense of inward spiritual condition, or to a lawlessness where almost anything goes unchallenged in the name of a "love" that judges nothing and disciplines no one.

"Brethren, the time is short." We surely feel like crying from the dust in the spirit of Nehemiah, "Lord, I and thy people have sinned." It is clearly time for us to humble ourselves personally and collectively under the mighty hand of God, peradventure He may show us mercy and give us a little reviving again in our day.

Let us raise the standard of loyalty to Christ! Back to the Word of God! Back to divine principles! Back to prayer! Back to holy living! Back to the clear ring of the Old Gospel preached in the power of the Spirit, of the blood and the cross, of heaven and hellfire! Back to the claims of the cross in the believer's life!

Let us rebuild the family altars that have so long been broken down, and gather our children around the holy Word again. Let us quit ourselves like men to deal with issues and give clear direction to the flock of God. Let us burn some midnight oil and gather sustenance from the Word of God for the hungry. Let us sacrifice some recreation and visit the ailing and the heartsick to bring solace and comfort.

The war is on! The enemy has made great inroads. The flock is wounded and many are scattered. So soon our little day of service will be over. Then the opened books, the eyes of fire, the Divine appraisal!

Where are the men willing to enter into the sanctuary and lie in the dust of self-abasement and self-judgment? Where are the men who will come forth with the glow of God upon their lives, to speak for God, governed by His Holy Spirit and bowing without question to the authority of Scripture? Where are the men willing to make unpopular decisions, to be mocked by the ungodly and slandered by the carnal? Where are the men who will sow in tears that they might reap a harvest for God with eternal joy? Where are those men? Let them come and let them come now.

The Grief, the Grave, and the Glory

Weeper of Bethany!
Heal my poor heart,
How long Thou hast tarried
Thy help to impart.

Look on my sorrow, Lord,
Number my tears;
Move with Thy power,
Dispel all my fears.

Now Thou art come to me,
Too late to save;
All of my hope
Lies cold in the grave.

Wonder of Bethany!
Giver of life!
Why did I doubt Thee,
When darkness was rife?

Worker of miracles!
Now I can see,
My sorrow's real purpose
Was glory for Thee!

Nevertheless Afterward

This day before the sun goes down, in many lands the anguished cry, "Why, O why?" will rise like Noah's dove into what seems to be an unresponsive and foreboding sky, only to return without a leaf of hope.

The infant son of a lovely Christian couple goes missing and the little form is later found floating at the bottom of a swimming pool. A beautiful young sister is abducted from the street, assaulted and killed, and the perpetrators of this monstrous act are never apprehended. A young husband, driving home from a conference, is killed by a drunken driver. A successful businessman, saved later in life, dedicates his experience to help the Lord's workers. He severs profitable connections on the basis of his newfound principles. He turns down lucrative business because his services would indirectly be used by his customers to produce materials that would grieve his Lord and violate his sense of decency. He suffers major financial losses.

A quick and easy answer to such sufferers would only be a mockery. To toss out a piece of sentimental poetry or quote a truth never experienced by the well-intentioned consoler would be unfeeling and thoughtless.

A cheery shout down into the pit, calling Joseph to "Have a good day!" would hardly have comforted this young man. *But the Lord had a plan for his release.* Though he may not have felt it, "the Lord was with him" and there was "nevertheless" a wonderful "afterward."

Job's three friends did visit him when he lost everything. Yet their words only served to plunge Job deeper into despair. *But the Lord had a plan for his restoration.* For Job, that meant a wonderful turn of events, and for God's people a commentary on the mystery of suffering, the ministry of the Lord and the maliciousness of Satan.

Jonah sinned by disobedience. Off he goes to escape his responsibility. *But the Lord had a plan for his recovery.* Not quite what Jonah expected. Miraculously, a wind, a whale and a weed were prepared, all to teach His failing servant a lesson on the great value of souls to God. Then, where sin abounded, grace did much more abound and he became the only sign the Saviour would ever give to His enemies, of His death, burial and resurrection.

What words could ever have brought comfort to that bereaved home in Bethany? What answers for the helplessness of watching their beloved brother slipping away while anguished prayers seemingly were not being heard? Death breaks in at last and in Bethany can be heard the moan of the mourning and the sob of the sorrowing. Why did the Lord not come? *But the Lord had a plan for a resurrection!* Mary and Martha so urgently wanted a miracle, a sick Lazarus kept alive. But far above and beyond the uncertain pulse of little Bethany, the tears of weeping sisters and a corrupting corpse in the grave, there was an eternal purpose, the glory of the Son of God and a new life to many who would believe.

Well and good, those incidents do throw a shaft of light in our darkness . . . at times, but there are sorrows, tragedies, personal pains and perplexities that seemingly have no answer down here. Some burst into our blue skies like a hurricane and leave us desolate in the ruins of all our hopes. Others with slow attrition gnaw at our endurance, draw daily upon the emotions and drain the strength from our will and our questionings afflict us with guilt.

What now? Does the Lord have a wonderful plan for me? No Joseph nor Jonah, no Martha nor Mary here, just one of the "nobodies" of life. Yes, dear saint in the trial, the Lord does have a plan, not necessarily for release, restoration or recovery, *but the Lord has a plan for reward.*

The answer for many sorrows will never be found down here. Though "manifold" be the trial, it is not forever, it is "for a season." The trial is temporal. In God's mysterious dealings with us, the trial is needful, "if need be." In the balances of eternity, the trial is valuable, "more precious than of gold that perisheth."

All who have thus suffered the trial of their faith, not only by pain and distress, but also by patient endurance, will receive "praise", the divine approbation. They will be given "honour," a suitable reward and they will be granted the radiant "glory" of a reigning rank in the kingdom of the Lord in whose Name they suffered and for whose sake they endured.

Fear of Silence

Everywhere they can be seen, heads bobbing, shoulders pointing, toes tapping, fingers drumming. They come in all sizes, shapes and styles. Male or female, young or old, they can be found almost anywhere, jogging in the park, sitting in the airport, on the way to school, or just gazing out there—somewhere. They have one thing in common, those little earphones, attached by an umbilical wire to a miniature tape recorder fastened to a belt or tucked in a pocket.

Their musical interest may vary from Brahms to the most raucous beat of hammering Rock. Of course there are spiritual songs and even the beauty of the spoken Scriptures to be heard by this device, so it can't be all bad—can it?

Well, one has to wonder whatever happened to silence? Are we afraid of it? Don't we know what to do in the silence? Think? Remember? Meditate? These can be troublesome exercises for some. So, "click," on goes the music, up goes the volume, and the product of other minds and voices pour into the lifelong memory banks of the brain. But is silence really silent?

I knew a brother who would take his grandchildren into the woods, sit them on a stump and tell them to "listen to the silence." He'd ask them what they heard. Their first answer was "Nothing." But soon they began to pick up a gentle symphony of seldom-noticed sounds. The crackling of twigs, the ruffling of the breeze through the leaves, the buzz of a passing insect, even the beating of their own hearts. So even in the "silence" we can learn that there is a sound to stillness.

Elijah discovered this. He had won a victory at Carmel and the fire from heaven testified who was the true God and who was His servant. Then there was Jezebel, who threatened the prophet with death on the morrow. The record states, "When he saw that, he arose and went for his life."

The Lord met him at Horeb and called him to stand on the mount. Then came the great wind, an earthquake, and a burning fire. But the Lord was not in these. Then we read "after the fire a still small voice" or, "the sound of a gentle stillness."

God had worked by fire at Carmel, but in spite of this, there was still no revival in Israel. "When he *saw* that . . ." (not *heard* that—for Elijah wasn't afraid of wicked Jezebel; he was discouraged at the lack of response to God) he fled "for his life." Not to save his life in fear, but to lay it down as finished, useless and hopeless in despair. Then the Lord taught him that in spite of the fact that nothing appears to be happening, God was there in the "sound of a gentle stillness."

So it seems, for some well-intentioned but mistaken believers today, that if there is no "activity," no "excitement," no outward display, they think God is not at work and all is at a standstill. Instead of the quietness of faith that can listen to the "still small voice," up jumps the agitated flesh that endeavors by novel programs, new methods, and worldly presentations, to produce an artificial earthquake, a bombastic wind, and a strange fire to get the attention of the people and make it appear that God is at work.

God is indeed at work, but quietly, in the individual lives of the saints. He is at work in the silent tear of the sorrowing, the quiet handshake of a restored brother, the sigh of the longing soul, the prayers of the intercessor, the burning of the midnight oil to discover the gold of God in His Word, and especially in the hidden growth of strengthened spirits that silently root ever deeper into the love of Christ.

Dear weary servant, because God is not shaking and burning and blasting, it does not mean He is not at work. His mightiest works have been done in the silence. Behold Calvary's three dark hours. If your work is not growing as you think it should, and you have done your part faithfully, it may be the time of the quiet work of God out of sight, rooting and grounding the saints in love.

Resist the temptation to follow those who crave for crowds, talk "excitement," organize big affairs, advertise, magnetize, socialize. Don't be afraid of the silent times.

Speak, Lord, in the stillness,
While I wait on Thee;
Hushed my heart to listen
In expectancy. —E. May Grimes

"Broken Noses

"N ow, we mustn't judge!" we occasionally hear in somewhat pious tones. This is usually followed by a quotation from Scripture that affirms we must not judge our brother. Yet spiritual intelligence and good sense in the things of God demand that we exercise certain judgments. How can we reconcile these two ideas?

By a mistaken notion of what it means to judge, errors may be permitted to creep into the fellowship of believers with tragic results. Sin may go unjudged and God's assembly may become prey to unscrupulous persons and harmful ministries. All this in the name of Christ, love, and a generous spirit.

The judgment we are not to engage in is that of arrogating to ourselves the position of passing sentence on a brother or sister *apart from the Word of God.* We are called upon to exercise judgment by applying scriptural principles to expose error, test values, or evaluate ministry. This kind of judgment does not in fact arise from us, but out of the Word of God; and when we do apply divine principles, it is not we who judge, but God.

It will be noted that we are enjoined to judge in certain areas. In 1 Corinthians 2:15, those who are spiritual judge all things—that is, to examine all things to discover their true nature. The idea of the word is to set a thing up for examination. Here the spiritual believer is seen as *a discerner.* If there is one ability that seems to be needed among us today, it is that of discernment. Sad to say, even among some who take a place of leadership, there is little or no discernment as to what is proper and profitable in the house of God. One thing that disqualified a priest in the old economy was a broken nose. The nose is the organ of discernment. The garlic of Egypt and the incense of the sanctuary bore little difference to the flat-nosed Israelite.

In 1 Corinthians 14:29, the listeners to the ministry of the Word are to judge. Here the idea is to *discriminate,* to make a distinction, to differentiate. Like the Bereans, who tested the ministry of Paul by the Word of God, believers are to "taste" the ministry of the Word and "test" it with godly discrimination to see what is of God and what is of man. Every minister must be prepared to have his ministry tested by the Scriptures. If this was the rule perhaps we would exercise more care as to the quality of ministry we would give.

In 1 Corinthians 6:2-5, there is the provision for a brother to judge, as *a mediator* in a dispute between brethren to resolve some difficulty rather than to go before the ungodly in a law court.

Believers are prayed for by Paul in Philippians 1:9 that they may abound in the realm of love. This love will manifest itself in a growing knowledge and with *spiritual intelligence* enable one to make correct moral decisions with a keen perception of what is right.

One of the characteristics of those who are mature spiritually is that the organs of spiritual perception are trained by careful exercise and a healthy spiritual diet so that they can judge between good and evil. Good judgment in this sense is one of the marks of *maturity* in Hebrews 5:14. To judge nothing and love everything, is not at all a mark of Christian love and generosity, but an exposure of milk-fed immaturity.

The child of God is cautioned in 1 John 4:1 not to accept every spirit as from God, but to prove them. That is to "put to the test," "to examine." It is evident that not everything that takes the name of Christ, or the Gospel or quotes the Bible is necessarily of God. As false teachers arise and as great claims are made, as super-slick presentations flood the media, it is incumbent on all true followers of the Lord Jesus Christ to judge as *testers* and prove what is of God and what is not.

We can see then, that far from saying we must not judge, we are enjoined to do so in the following ways:

Hypocritical judging is forbidden (Mt. 7:1-5)
Superficial judging is forbidden (Jn. 7:24)
Judging by the unconfessedly guilty is forbidden (Jn. 8:7)
Judging that stumbles a brother is forbidden (Rom. 14:13)
Judging of hidden motives and counsels is forbidden (1 Cor. 4:5)
Judgment that is evil-speaking is forbidden (Jas. 4:11)
The spiritual will judge all things to *discern* true character (1 Cor. 2:12)
A brother may judge as *a mediator* between brethren (1 Cor. 6:2-5)
Listening believers are to be *discriminators* of ministry given (1 Cor. 14:29)
Charitable believers will manifest their love with *intelligence,* making correct moral decisions (Phil. 1:9)
Mature believers evidence their development by discerning between good and evil (Heb. 5:14)
Children of God are to be aware of false spirits and judge as *testers* where the truth lies (1 Jn. 4:1).

God Our Saviour

Thou God all transcending,
Of life never ending,
The Source, in whose hand is the key;
The only inscrutable,
Ever immutable;
Broken hearts mending,
To feeblest cry bending,
In love Thy Son sending
To save a poor sinner like me.

O God all pervading,
Of glory unfading,
Who art Thine own vast dwelling place;
Thou God of antiquity,
Far-flung ubiquity;
Hell's hosts invading,
Their prisoners aiding;
In Secret Place shading
The weary, who rest in Thy grace.

O God, praise is blending,
And worship ascending;
Thy Majesty burns as a flame
Of Light unapproachable,
Rights unencroachable;
Yet condescending
The wanderer tending,
The Comforter sending
To all who have called on Thy Name.

The First

Fear of the unknown touches the souls of some on occasions. Perhaps more at the beginning of the year than at other times. Whatever lies before us in the days ahead their content is all unknown to us. For some this kind of uncertainty has always been a cause for concern. So much so that necromancy and astrological hocus-pocus are offered daily in the media to be swallowed by the simple and digested by the deluded as a prescription for promised peace of mind. This fear and unrest is not a new thing for we read in a very ancient Book ". . . the misery of man is great upon him. For he knoweth not that which shall be" (Eccl. 8:7).

The believer in Christ, however, need not be discomfited by such fears for while the way ahead is all unknown to us, it is written of our God, that "He knoweth what is in the darkness."

John on Patmos fell as dead at the unveiling of the glorified Lord. The Lord gave John that day and all of us a revelation of Himself that should forever remove our fears, the fears of living, fears of dying, and fears of eternal existence. He said to John, "Fear not."

Stepping into the year ahead we can do so in absolute peace and confidence as we hear our Lord and Saviour say, "Fear not; I am the First." An apprehension of this great fact will deliver us from the fear of the unknown pathway ahead.

He is first in point of time. Time comes out of the future, we come out of the past and we meet time at that ever-moving point we call present. As time creatures we must wait the rising of the sun to reach tomorrow. The Lord transcends time. He is not bound to the procession of the clock. He is above the sun. With Him there is neither "tomorrow" nor "yesterday" as we perceive them. He is the One who inhabits eternity and He is already in all our tomorrows. He could say, "My sheep hear My voice and I know them and they follow Me." The Good Shepherd is already up ahead making sure that the road is not too steep and the path is not too rough for the sheep to bear. Fear not; He is first in point of time and He undertakes.

He is first in order of experience. He is first in sorrow. There is not a shadow in the valley He does not know. There is not a pain in the heart He has not felt, sin apart. As the Man of Sorrows there was no sorrow like unto His sorrow. He has drained the bitter cup and nothing we may face will take Him by surprise nor be beyond His balm to comfort or His power to heal.

He is first in suffering. Pain is part of this mortal experience but no one has suffered as did He. While we may know some mortal pain in days ahead, all the pains of hell gat hold on Him in concentrated anguish. There is no pain to which He is a stranger, sin apart. While others may stand by in helplessness there will always be One who can fully sympathize and mightily relieve.

He is first in temptation. While our beloved Lord is the Impeccable One and could not sin, He was tempted in all points like as we are, sin apart. His sinless character and holy nature did not make temptation more palatable for Him but more painful. Our calloused souls, our comfortable consciences and constricted visions have dulled our sensitivities to the tragedy of sin to moral dangers and distance from God. Not so the Holy One. He has known the blast of the terrible one and was victorious. He is first in order of experience and He understands.

He is first in order of rank. There is none *higher* than He. He sits in the place of zenith glory "far above all." Therefore all *things* are under His feet. There is none *greater* than He. He has "gone into heaven and is on the right hand of God; angels and authorities and powers being made subject unto Him." Therefore all *authority* is in His hand. There is none *mightier* than He. In the shadows of the cross "He knew that all things were delivered into His hands." Therefore all *circumstances* are under His control. He is first in order of rank and overrules.

He overshadows His people with His protection. He undergirds them with His strength. He goes before them to keep them in the way. He comes behind them as a rearward against the last attacks of the enemy. He enters in and takes up residence within the believing heart. "Fear not."

Faint not, Christian! though the road leading to thy blest abode
Darksome be, and dangerous too; Christ, thy Guide, will bring thee through.
—James H. Evans

The Last

I n a day when it is perceived to be quite the clever thing to overlook, overrule, or overthrow authority, and when every form of rule and order is being challenged, whether in the home, the church or the state, it is most fitting that those who name the name of Christ as Saviour and Lord should be confirmed in their conviction that there is one final authority, superseding all others, overruling all others, and, therefore, demanding a wise and worthy response of glad submission and joyous obedience from everyone.

We note the words of the Lord to John on Patmos, "Fear not; I am the First . . ." An apprehension of this singular ascription was seen to deliver the believer in Christ from fears of the unknown path ahead, the uncontrollable powers around and the unanswerable problems within. Now the Lord Jesus reveals Himself as "The Last" (Rev. 1:17).

He is the Last as the culmination of all things. All things are moving *towards* Him as the ultimate objective of the universe. The procession of time, the sweep of civilization, the rise and fall of nations, the slow wheeling of the galaxies, the armies of heaven, of earth and of hell, are all, by divine compulsion, converging towards one point, and that, the once-pierced feet of the Lord of Glory. He is the great unavoidable. We may meet Him now by grace, through faith, unto salvation. Or we can reject Him now and meet Him later at the great white throne of judgment from which there is no escape.

There will come a moment when, in the Name of Jesus, every knee will bow to the highly exalted One. Then for once in the history of realms celestial, realms terrestrial and realms infernal there will be perfect harmony. From every throat will burst forth the ascription, "He is Lord," and God the Father will be glorified, God the Son will be magnified, and God the Holy Spirit will be satisfied.

The Lord Jesus is the Last also as the controller of all things. All things are moved *by* Him as the final authority of the universe. We discover in Colossians 1:16 that "all things were created by Him." Not only is He the beginning of everything that had a beginning, He is the upholder of all things that exist. He is the sovereign sustainer of the universe and none can wrest that authority from His hand.

Scientists speak of our universe as expanding, where the stars are receding at the speed of light. They tell us that the atoms by the same laws *should* be flying apart, but some power, they call "the great force" holds them together. Their calculations alarm them, their observations confound them, their impotence frustrates them and they wonder where it is all going to end. The believer in Christ rests in this, Jesus said, "I am the Last" and all is under His control. While things so often seem to be out of man's control, nothing ever escapes His ultimate authority. So the Bible declares, "Jesus Christ: who is gone into heaven, and is on the right hand of God; angels and authorities and powers being made subject unto Him" (1 Pet. 3:22).

This glorious One is also the Last as the consummation of all things. All things are moving *for* Him as the completed purpose of God. Colossians 1:16 declares, "All things were created . . . for Him." E. W. Bullinger, in *The Witness of the Stars,* shows that on the fourteenth day of the month Nisan on the Hebrew calendar (Passover), in the year of the crucifixion, "the sun stood at the very spot marked by the stars El Nath (the pierced, the wounded or slain), and Al Sheratan (the bruised, or wounded)"! When earth had rejected the Lord from heaven, His celestial creation witnessed for Him, and to Him, as the Lamb of God who was "wounded for our transgressions" (Isa. 53:5). The calendar in the skies testified in silent dignity that "in due time Christ died for the ungodly." God has declared that "He hath purposed in Himself: That in the dispensation of the fullness of times He might gather together in one, all things in Christ, both which are in heaven, and which are on earth; even in Him" (Eph. 1:9-10).

This is the One of whom the Scriptures speak, of whom the heavens declare and concerning whom the Father commands "Hear ye Him." He will have the last word in everything.

True image of the Infinite, Whose essence is concealed;
Brightness of uncreated light, the heart of God revealed.
But the high mysteries of His Name the creature's grasp transcend;
The Father only (glorious claim!) the Son can comprehend
Worthy, O Lamb of God, art Thou, that every knee to Thee should bow.
—J. Conder

Unknown Soldiers

Lying among the noble and renowned in Westminster Abbey is the body of the Unknown Soldier, placed there because he gave his life for his country and represents all who fell in battle. Honoured but unknown.

Recently I had the sad privilege of following in the funeral cortege of a beloved brother and true friend of many years. Outside of a few Ontario assemblies, brother Sam was virtually unknown. As we passed along, I could not help but think that the Lord gave us a glimpse of His appreciation for His saints, "of whom the world (is) not worthy."

Yonge Street is the main artery of Toronto going north from the heart of the city. Bustling with traffic, crowded with pedestrians, traffic signals blink their red eyes at every block. The long line of funeral cars was shepherded through this maze by four motorbike police who, with remarkable dexterity, replaced one another at each corner and halted all traffic at every intersection so that the funeral procession could proceed together.

I watched the traffic of this great city being stopped and the people on the sidewalk turning to watch, and no doubt to wonder who this was being carried to the burial. I could not help but smile at the thought of my beloved brother, a gentle, quiet and unassuming Irishman, who sought only to please the Lord and serve His people, and who coveted neither place nor attention in this world—here he was, bringing the traffic of this great city to a standstill as his mortal remains passed on to their last resting place to await the enlivening shout.

Well, after all, by the grace of God he, and all who love the Lord, will yet sing unto "Him that loved us, and washed us from our sins in His own blood, and hath made us kings and priests unto God . . ." While on earth, my brother in Christ belonged to the vast army of the unknown in this world. The saints are nevertheless of the blood royal, princes of the realm, and will yet be administrators for the King of kings, and judges of angels. They will accompany the Lord of lords when He appears to this world again to set up that longed-for kingdom on earth.

Then those honoured, unknown soldiers whose battalions fired no guns, whose Sword drew no blood, whose decorations were meekness and Christlikeness, who wore their wounds for Christ as badges of honour, will enter into the realization of the third beatitude and inherit the earth in the Lord's Name. They will appear with Him, and their sufferings endured in faith will have been transfigured into a radiant glory. Unknown they were on earth, but well known on the battlements of heaven.

Of the increase of the government of this King there will be no end. He will forever extend the coastlines of His everlasting empires and, as the Creator still, will doubtless bring into existence sinless beings to inhabit those unnumbered island universes, which were created not in vain.

In those far-flung territories, untold hosts on hosts must hear the strains of the everlasting Gospel, not now to the saving of sinners, for sin has been forever put away by the blood of the King once rejected, but to the glory of the Saviour as He is magnified by every creature. Oh, to be an evangelist then! With a retinue of ministering angels to declare His glory and mighty accomplishments at a place called Calvary on planet Earth! The vastness of His kingdom will resound with cadences of music undreamed of by the composers of earth. Harmonies unknown in this vale of tears will fill the endless halls of heavenly realms.

Hallelujahs to His honour will ascend in volume like the "voice of many waters and as the voice of mighty thunderings" from every direction in the infinities of the spatial heavens. Their theme will be the praise of Him—Saviour, Redeemer, King—for what He accomplished for the glory of the Father, and for its inhabitants, this race of sinners, that He loved beyond measure.

Well, brother Sam, they didn't know you on Yonge Street. To them, you were an unknown, passing quietly by in the black limousine. An unknown soldier, who with countless others make up the silent army that is being gathered home day by day for a great review, a wondrous celebration of love, and then to join the mighty, invincible force that will follow the King of kings back to earth. Not then will they carry their cross and the burden of an ailing mortality, but they will bear His likeness, and carry His Name as a diadem of beauty in their foreheads and a badge of authority in His eternal service.

Unknown soldiers? Yes, on earth, but renowned in heaven and inscribed in the Lamb's Book of Life!

Let such as know no second birth labour to write their names on earth;
My joy is this, that love divine on heaven's scroll has written mine. —W. Blane

The Battle

Ever since Cain rose up and killed his brother, the pages of human history have been stained with the blood of victims, the blood of the innocents, the blood of armies. The flower of the human race has been cut down on the battlefields of this old world, and nations have sung their plaintive songs to lament the tragedy of war. Yet still we will struggle with one another, still we devise weapons of mass destruction to slaughter human beings who were created for an eternal purpose and for God's glory (Isa. 43:7).

As we review this sad history and hear the generals count corpses by percentages of loss, mothers and wives and children wring from their souls the bitter tears no victory can assuage and no conquest can comfort. We must surely conclude there is something fundamentally wrong with the human race. What hellish alchemy is it that can transform plain people into sworn enemies? In tranquil times, men and women can laugh together, weep together, learn one another's languages to converse together about the things we hold in common, then at some strident trumpet call, don uniforms, take up weapons and be ready to blast the life from one another's heart? What is it?

We hear much at the time of this writing about "The Mother of all Battles." Well, we have a description of the Father of Battles in Revelation 19. At last the united nations will form one vast army of coalition. Not now to fight one another, but to fight against God and His people. For once the armies of earth will be united without a dissenting voice (Isa. 59:16). Through the ages, armies have gone to war singing their battle-hymns, all claiming God was on their side. Their belt buckles, their streaming colours declare "God with us," "For God and Country," and so on. Now what will they do? For their battle is with God.

Up to this point in history, the armies of heaven have been for the most part silent and invisible. This concealment however has not been for strategy, but for mercy. Occasionally an advance patrol has been permitted to break through the veil of invisibility and penetrate the encampment of time. These occasions give a faint glimpse of the might of heaven's host. In 2 Kings 19:35, one single angelic warrior smote 185,000 Assyrians in a night! And without a weapon!

Now with weapons trained, nuclear warheads armed, armies, navies and air forces, under a central command, in eerie quietness the nations await the advancing armies of the rejected God. Suddenly heaven opens! Here they come in glittering array! Leading His combined forces is the Lord Himself! Swiftly and silently as light, the armies of earth are overshadowed and surrounded. The mighty Conqueror comes—and who is He? The revelation of this One shocks the earth. It is JESUS! Not now the Man of Sorrows dressed in the homespun of a carpenter of Nazareth. He comes, not to speak peace as He did before, but to "judge and make war" (Rev. 19:11). He is at the same time the "Faithful and True" witness against the rebel race and the Judge of the Supreme Court of the universe where there are no parolees and no suspended sentences! He brings the incriminating evidence to this military court, "A vesture dipped in blood" (v. 13) and all shall see His names emblazoned upon His person and His garment of glory, "King of kings and Lord of lords."

He will need no guns, nor bombs to subdue mans' rebel force. He will but speak one word from His mouth and as a sharp sword it will smite His enemies in a moment (v. 15).

But He had fought a greater battle. The Battle of all Battles, and He fought it single-handedly. He didn't look like a king that day, crowned with thorns, anointed with spittle. The one swordsman who had tried clumsily to defend Him had fled, and the enemy took Him and nailed Him to a cross. Yet the paradox was that the armies of Heaven were at His command! He said that He could have called twelve legions of angels, but He had not come to judge the world, He had come to save. He entered into that fierce conflict to deal with your sins and mine. There, alone in the darkness "He was wounded for our transgressions, He was bruised for our iniquities . . ." and there He died, *a King crucified, to save a poor sinner like me.* He conquered death and rose again, to be a living Saviour to all who will receive Him by faith (Jn. 1:11-12).

That brings us to the Battle of the Human Heart! God calls us all to bow the knee to this rejected King now, to trust Him for the forgiveness of our sins. If we will obey, He will save us and we will be numbered among His own who will never perish. Then on that great day of judgment and battle, you will be among the armies of heaven, not vainly hiding under the naked camouflage of man's devices only to perish at the last.

Our Lord is now rejected, and by the world disowned, by the many still neglected, and by the few enthroned;
But soon He'll come in glory! The hour is drawing nigh, For the crowning day is coming by and by. —D.W.Whittle

Circumstance

It was not planned this way,
This lowly task;
It's dread monotony
I did not ask.
Great things I meant to dare and do,
Numbered with the noble few,
Until I saw advance, with dreadful retinue
The force of Circumstance.

'Twas not in all my sight;
This lonely room
Would bind my wing from flight.
Yet in the gloom,
As tho' to mock this weakened frame,
The mind with purpose is aflame,
And seeks for one on whom to blame
The fault of Circumstance.

It shall NOT conquer me,
This lurking foe;
I'll smite the enemy
With killing blow;
Yet as I rise to do or die,
I see his cohorts riding high,
Outweighed! O'er whelmed! too weak am I
To fight my Circumstance.

Oh, had I dove-like wing,
This lurid nest
I'd soar above, to sing
And be at rest;
But even as I think to flee,
I see the bonds that fasten me
To this impossibility,
No flight from Circumstance.

Deep darkness chills the soul,
And lightnings scar
The heavens, and thunders roll,
No sun—no star,
The tempest steals my frightened cry,
Tremble to live, nor want to die,
"Eli lama Sabachthani"
I fear this Circumstance.

"Ah, child, thou'rt ever Mine,
Belov'd alway,
The sun, the stars still shine
Above the fray;
Thy darkness hideth not from Me,
My Spirit moves to comfort thee,
My priestly voice presents thy plea:
Have faith, in this, thy Circumstance."

Beauty for Ashes

It has been the longing of men from antiquity to be able to start over again. In the ancient city of On, the people worshipped their idea of this—Phoenix, the mythical bird that lived in the Arabian desert and every few centuries burnt itself on a funeral pyre, then rose from the ashes to begin another cycle. It has been the desire and dream of poets:

> *"I wish that there were some wonderful place*
> *Called the "Land of Beginning again,"*
> *Where all our mistakes, and all our heartaches,*
> *And all of the poor selfish griefs,*
> *Could be dropped like a shabby old coat at the door,*
> *And never be put on again."*

There are some even among the Lord's people whose dreams have turned to ashes. The plans they set out to fulfill a year ago either never crystallized or crumbled before their eyes as they suffered the shock of disastrous reverses in the economy. Others with noble aspirations for their own spiritual lives look back on failures and the enemy loves to have it so.

Our God is the God of recovery, the God of restoration, the God of new beginnings. Failure is not final! The God of all grace has given us many examples of this in the Scriptures. Poor Israel is one. Shattered and scattered, plundered and punished she is seen in Isaiah 59 separated by her sins from the fellowship of God. She sits in the ashes of despair mourning as a dove and roaring like a bear, abandoned and without a friend in all the world to plead her cause. Even God wonders that there is no intercessor. She is about to be inundated by the enemy pouring in like a swirling flood. Everything and everyone wherein she had trusted has failed and great tribulation seems as though it will utterly destroy her. Then! Suddenly it will happen! The heavens so long silent will open and the Spirit of the Lord will raise up a standard against all her enemies. Her Redeemer shall come to Zion, not then in lowliness but Lordly glory; not then to Gabbatha and Golgotha, but to glorify and be glorified. He sends forth His word of light for her darkness and hope for her despair. He appoints a time and a place to make some wonderful exchanges!

For the ashes of Israel's earthly dreams He offers the cosmetic of heavenly beauty. For the empty vessels of their mourning, be they ever so many, He will fill them with the oil of joy from a cruse that will never fail. For the leaden weights that have burdened their heavy spirits for so long He will give them the wings of praise so that they shall mount up and soar as eagles in heavenly heights. The veil will drop from their eyes, and that people who have not desired Him—for they saw no beauty in Him—may well exclaim, "Yea, He is altogether lovely!"

So it was also with suffering Job. At last he came forth from the furnace and cried out "I repent in dust and ashes" and turned his face, wet with tears and covered in ashes upward to his God, his Vindicator. The God of the New Beginning would not refuse such a look. "The Lord accepted *the face* of Job" and restored him his ministry, his liberty, his hospitality and his prosperity including three lovely daughters. Job named them as a living testimony and constant reminder of the God who delights to restore. Kerenhappuch "a vial of cosmetics". She was Beauty for his ashes. Kezia, means "Cassia." She was the fragrant Oil of Joy for his mourning. Jemima means "dove" the bird of mourning and of peace. She was the Garment of Praise for his spirit of heaviness.

Many sit among the ashes of remorse for past sins and failures. There is a mourning over losses that seem so final. There is heaviness of many a spirit that has silenced the song and quenched the joy. The enemy would have us sit there and mourn over the past, but hear this! "He restoreth my soul." If there has been sin, confess it and fall back into the arms of His Grace rejoicing in the value of the blood of Christ. If restitution can be made, let us do it. If wounded and misjudged, commit it to Him. If bereft of means or a loved one gone, hear Him say, "Bring Me your grief, your groans and your graves, and leave them all with Me; in exchange I will give you My beauty, My joy, and a spirit exulting in praise."

> *Ye fearful saints fresh courage take, the clouds ye so much dread*
> *Are big with mercy and will break with blessing on your head.* —William Cowper

Heartaches

There is a pain no medicine can cure and no surgeon can cut out. Multitudes in our day suffer from it. The people of God are not immune. It is the pain of the aching heart.

David Livingstone recorded in his diary: "The strangest disease I have found in this country seems really to be brokenheartedness." Speaking of many who died without any visible malady, he said, "They express surprise that they should die . . . it seems really to be broken hearts of which they expire."

None are excluded from this pain. The young have it as well as the old. The rich, having every material comfort lie down with the burdened poor in this sad sickness. Carnal believers suffer from it and deeply spiritual saints have groaned with the sorrow of it. There seems to be hardly a home without its intrusion. It is the pervading pain of the twentieth century. This writer in recent days has heard little children weep for separated parents, young people sob for the lonely lack of a true friend, and young couples despairing as their dreams crumble before them. He has visited businessmen who groan under crushing financial blows, parents shattered by family catastrophes and seen beloved servants of God weeping over their children.

In the history of the Church, it seems that Satan attacked the bodies of the saints with fire and sword. In our day, it is the heart and its affections and the mind and its attentions he is after. If only he can distract the people of God and divert them away from Christ, he will employ any means to do so. He will try to crush them with sorrow, blind them with tears and burden them with care. He will grind them with pressure from every direction at once and mock at their weakness, snarling into their darkness, "Where is now thy God?"

Well, where is He? Is He indeed a distant deity, an uncaring despot leaving us to find our own answers and produce our own healing? Ah, no! "He healeth the broken in heart, and bindeth up their wounds. He telleth the number of the stars; and calleth them all by their names" (Ps. 147:3-4). This gives the lie to the evil insinuation that our God is uncaring and our case is impossible. God cares and God can!

The tender Man of Sorrows cares. It is one of His anointed ministries "to heal the brokenhearted" (Lk. 4:18). The Holy Spirit cares. He makes intercession, translating the silent cry of the aching heart into the language of Heaven (Rom. 8:26-27). Yes, the enemy can wound and smite, oppress and mock, but over and above all is our risen Lord and even Satan is subject to Him (1 Pet. 3:22). When this time of testing passes, as it will, and the tear is dried we shall come forth as gold of the seventh refining.

We may never understand God's ways with us in this life but we can trust Him utterly to see us through the shadow into the sunshine and we shall laugh again with holy laughter at the bounty of His blessings.

Weary hearts! weary hearts! by cares of life oppressed,
Ye are wandering in the shadows, ye are sighing for the rest;
There is darkness in the heavens, and the earth is bleak below,
And the joys we taste today may tomorrow turn to woe. Weary hearts! God is rest.

Lonely hearts! lonely hearts! 'tis but a land of grief;
Ye are pining for repose, ye are longing for relief;
What the world hath never given, kneel and ask of God above,
And your grief shall turn to gladness if you lean upon His love. Lonely hearts! God is love.

Restless hearts! restless hearts! ye are toiling night and day,
And the flowers of life, all withered, leave but thorns along your way;
Ye are waiting, ye are waiting till your toilings here shall cease,
And your ever-restless throbbing is a sad, sad prayer for peace. Restless hearts! God is peace.

Broken hearts! broken hearts! ye are desolate and lone,
And low voices from the past o'er your present ruins moan;
In the sweetest of your pleasures there was bitterest alloy,
And a starless night hath followed on the sunset of your joy. Broken hearts! God is joy.

Homeless hearts! homeless hearts! through the dreary, dreary years,
Ye are lonely, lonely wanderers, and your way is wet with tears;
In bright or blighted places, wheresoever ye may roam,
Ye look away from earthland, and ye murmur, "Where is Home?" Homeless hearts! God is home. —F. Ryan

The Swordsmen

There were sixty of them. Men of great courage and utterly trustworthy. Each one had his own weapon at hand. They were called to take up a position in the dark because of fear in the night. They were Solomon's guard, set for the defense of the King's person in a time of danger.

Without being poetic, it is a time of spiritual darkness in the world. The word of Scripture is "The night is far spent." Soon the Lord will come and for the believer there will dawn a morning without a sunset. In the meantime, we all have an obligation of love, and that to defend the person of the King of kings.

The enemy is always on the move at night. Advancing here, strengthening a post there, setting forces in array for attack and destruction. Certainly his violence breaks through in places. He tears and bombards and blasts at every stronghold, seeking to terrify the defenders of Truth.

In the battle many of God's beloved are wounded. Many of God's assemblies are divided and debilitated. Yet they are not the real target of his furious crusade. It is God's King he seeks to attack. By incursion and invasion, overtly and covertly, his desire is to defame the Person of the King. He little cares what destruction he causes in the lives of those who love the Lord; that is incidental to his main campaign.

This wicked enemy attacks on all fronts. He attacks the eternal Sonship of our glorious Lord. He mocks at the reality of His miraculous conception and virgin birth. By vague and specious arguments, he would seek to rend that garment of glory, the hypostatic union of the "mystery of godliness: God . . . manifest in the flesh." Ever the thief, he seeks to rob our Lord of the attributes of deity while on earth and add insult to injury by misusing Scripture (his expertise) to claim our beloved Lord was capable of sinning. The cross does not escape the fury of his attack. He uses even good men, great men, to say that there are limits to His atoning work.

Much of this havoc sadly comes through Christendom itself, through men with false notions of loyalty and a pseudo-intellectualism that preens itself on the pinnacle of its ivory towers, far above the great unwashed masses. From the dark sewers of the filthy minds of the ungodly comes another attack. With the muck of their own depravity, they seek to despoil the holy, spotless character of our dear Saviour. Books and films are spewed out of their sickness that charge the Holy One of God with abominable sins like their own. His precious, holy Name is violated in blasphemy every day and in that sacred Name they damn their fellowmen to hell.

It is night; the darkness deepens. Where are the swordsmen, standing firm and expert in war? Could we, if called upon, take the Word and slice through the heresies with skill? Can we cut through the ungodly blasphemy of the wicked with the Sword of the Lord? Are we ready for the subtle intrusions of just "a little" error, to cut it open and expose it for what it really is? Elders, teachers, are you there? Are you aware? Are you ready to defend the King in the night? Not like Peter, however, slashing and hacking and cutting off ears, but with skill and expertise gained in the quiet place with God.

Sound the battle-cry! See! the foe is nigh;
Raise the standard high for the Lord;
Gird your armour on, stand firm, ev'ryone;
Rest your cause upon His holy Word.

Strong to meet the foe, marching on we go,
While our cause we know, must prevail;
Shield and banner bright, gleaming in the night;
Battling for the right, We ne'er can fail.

Oh! Thou God of all, hear us when we call;
Help us one and all, by Thy Grace;
When the battle's done, and the vict'ry won,
May we wear the crown, before Thy face.

Rouse, then, soldiers! Rally round the banner!
Ready, steady, pass the word along;
Onward, forward, shout aloud Hosanna!
Christ is Captain of the mighty throng. —Wm. F. Sherwin

The Winter is Past

It is a simply glorious day here in this part of Canada. The sunlight is streaming in through the study window. Winter's snow has capitulated at last and from where I sit I can see its last stubborn vestiges are in full retreat under the insistent barrage of the sun's warm and beneficent rays.

Here and there, as though to mock the winter's last stand, a few crocuses have broken out their colours. For so long they lay concealed here and there; some in clumps together and a few single bulbs in lonely shaded corners; silent, unlovely and imprisoned in the hard grip of the frozen earth.

The birds have congregated at the bird feeder as though to celebrate this sunny victory. Mostly sparrows, but one cardinal in ceremonial red, his throat swelling, sends out his lovely call above the chirping of the others.

The sun, the flowers and the birds are all united in an undeniable declaration, "The winter is past"! So many times this morning my mind has turned to the scripture from which these words are taken, ". . . lo, the winter is past, the rain is over and gone; the flowers appear on the earth; the time of the singing of the birds is come . . . Arise, my love, my fair one, and come away" (Song of Sol. 2:10-13).

In the chronology of God, since His dear Son gave His life for sinners, then arose from the dead and returned to Heaven, it has been a day of His grace for this troubled world. The gospel of the glory of the blessed God has called and still calls sinners to repentance and faith, that they might be saved.

For the people of God it has been a long winter's night of waiting. The icy grip of this hard world seems to have the victory. But they are there! A few clumps here and there, and some, isolated in lonely corners. But they are there! With no special beauty, they lie concealed, waiting. A few green shoots can be seen, it is true, but that is not all that yet shall be.

One of these days it will happen! The heavenly Bridegroom will come for His bride and take her to the eternal Summerland. With no more indications than they have already, the believers in Christ, who form that Bride will hear His trumpet call, "Arise, my love, my fair one, and come away." Then in a moment, in the twinkling of an eye we shall be changed. The plain and unadorned, so long concealed in the potential of promise alone will burst forth in a blaze of beauty. Unspectacular saints hidden away in the shaded corners of life will suddenly be seen radiant in their God-given glory. Each will be uniquely beautiful and in exquisite harmony they will contribute to the beauty of each other and all together to the glory of their Beloved.

Then will The Song begin. The discord of sorrow and sighing will have no part in that heavenly composition. Sounds unearthly, harmonies unheard on earth, will pour forth in sweetest cadence and in thundering crescendos. Mighty hallelujahs will rise to "Him that loved us and loosed us from our sins."

The roseate hue of the light of the Lamb will bless our unclouded vision and illume by its shadowless rays, the wonders of heaven. Thus we shall never forget that every wonder we behold and every blessing we enjoy was made possible only by "the precious blood of Christ as of a Lamb without blemish and without spot."

Dear child of God, weary in the conflict, lonely or afraid and hurt by cold calamities, *faint not!* Life recedes, time speeds away, the body grows old but this is not all for us. Soon, soon, Jesus will come! Lift up your hearts! The morning without a cloud is about to dawn. The altogether lovely Bridegroom of our hearts is on the way. Listen for His footfall. His hand is on the door-latch! We see Him through the lattice! Soon we shall hear His voice—that beautiful voice— *"The winter is past . . . the flowers appear . . . the time of the singing is come . . . arise, my love, my fair one, and come away."*

Then we shall see His face and it will have been worth it all.

I Am He That Liveth

Today we said farewell to another of God's choice saints whose body has been the repository of the Holy Spirit for most of a long pilgrimage of 94 years. A mother in Israel, quiet and unassuming, her godly character—not her lips—told us all that she was no stranger to the holy place. I suppose we shall never know this side of the glory what we owe to her intercessions.

There are few places on earth quite like a graveyard; silent, dignified, still. As we stand there in the midst of the granite and marble harvest of the Grim Reaper, we are made to realize that this tragic tillage contains the concentrated dust of a thousand sorrows. It represents the pains of a thousand deaths and the pangs of as many broken hearts. It has mingled and drunk in the tears of the fatherless and the widow.

The gardener, like the cosmetician, has done his best with death to hide its horror and conceal its corruption with a superficial beauty. But as we walk slowly along its neatly ordered paths, lined by its much too tidy borders, we are all the time conscious of the fact that this is not the rest of victory, it is the silence of defeat.

Blow the trumpet over the grave if you will, cover it with the glory of the flag, smother the rude hole with floral tributes, but it is still defeat. For beneath this tidy well-trimmed sod, lie the bones of shattered hopes. Great plans for the future lie withered in the hollow silent breasts of men and women who discovered they had no future left on earth in which to implement their plans. Here lie dreams unfulfilled, joys untasted, debts unpaid, service unfinished.

A graveyard, by its very silence, is a frustrating piece of field. How many have cried into an open grave, "Why? Why? Why?" But the dumb dust could give no answer, for death is so final. It is so inevitably the end of this mortal life, the tragic terminus of our earthly sojourn. All we can do is turn at last with heavy heart and solemn step to eat the bread of sorrow and drink the cup of weeping.

At least, that is what it would be but for one thing, a voice, and what a voice! Speaking words, and what words! Words of hope, and what a hope! Words that shout victory over every graveyard and mock the bands of cruel death.

They are the words of the Son of God, "I am He that liveth, and was dead; and behold, I am alive forevermore, Amen" (Rev. 1:18). Here is glory in the graveyard! Here is triumph over the tomb. Here is the secret of song in the sepulcher, "O death, where is thy sting? O grave, where is thy victory?" (1 Cor. 15:55).

So these groans and bones and granite stones are not the end after all. There is One who has vanquished death and vacated the tomb and He has vouchsafed to everyone who trusts in Him that He will sweep from the graves the precious dust of His own and gather them in glittering array before Him in bodies like unto His body of glory.

As the One who plundered death of its terrors, He knows every attack of the enemy in that cold, dark realm and says to His own, "Fear not . . . I was dead." As the One who sank to the very bottom under billows of pain and anguish, He can say, "Fear not . . . I was *dead*." As the One who knows every shadow in the valley and has banished the darkness of the tomb, He says, "Fear not . . . I *was* dead; and, behold, I am alive forevermore."

> *"Death could not keep its prey, Jesus my Saviour,*
> *He tore the bars away, Jesus my Lord."*

As the Living One, His people are assured that they are forever united to a real person, not some nebulous ghost as heretics preach. Not only living, but living *within* every child of God (Jn. 14:23; Rev. 3:20). We do not try to explain it, but we thoroughly believe His Word. As the Living One, His people are assured that they may ever enjoy His real presence dwelling in their hearts (Eph. 3:17; Heb. 13:5). As the Living One, His people are assured that they may ever derive real power from Him for any exigency (Eph. 1:19-20). That is the very power with which Christ was raised from the dead.

> *He lives! He lives! What glorious consolation!*
> *Exalted at His Father's own right hand;*
> *He pleads for us, and by His intercession,*
> *Enables all His saints by grace to stand.* —C. R. Hurditch

Forevermore, Amen

Eternity! What an awesome thought! Unending perpetuity, never ever coming to an end. When ten billion ages have rolled their course, still it is on and on and on into the vanishing point of eternal days, never, never ceasing to exist.

The Lord deals with fear by the unveiling of certain great facts of His personal glory. Not the fear of the Lord, but fears of the invisible, the incomprehensible, the infinite.

When we think of eternal existence it can be awesome indeed. For some, the thought of unending perpetuity might even touch the soul with fear.

For the Christ rejecter, of course, well may they fear an interminable existence, shut out from God, as eternal nonentities with neither name nor number. Many of these falsely assume that, though rejecting the only way of salvation from sin, nevertheless they will be gathered by a beneficent deity into His holy heaven at the last. How utterly foolish and unbiblical is this notion. Why should it be thought a thing incredible that God, holy and just, should not give rebellious sinners the extension of their own choice, no God—*forever?* These choose to live without God, to violate His holy laws and deny His gracious provision of a Saviour, the Lord Jesus. They live for self and for this world, thus they make their own choice to have no God—forever.

Dear reader, if this is your case, well might you fear your latest breath. Then, a captive of the last enemy, you will be ushered through the dark portals of a lonely death into the bottomless deeps of your chosen perdition *forever!*

But the gospel declares that there is still time and opportunity to escape. Turn to Christ, who died for the ungodly. Turn from all your idols and your toys of dust. Come and receive Him by faith as the only Saviour from sin and He will keep His Word, "Him that cometh to Me I will in no wise cast out" (Jn. 6:37). He will save you and give you everlasting life (Rom. 6:23).

For the believer in Christ, that word "forevermore" may cause a sense of awe and wonder but it need cause no qualms. Paul speaks of "the ages that are coming" when God, rich in mercy and great in love, will display to wondering angels, the exceeding riches of His grace by being kind toward His own through Christ Jesus (Eph. 2:7). FOREVERMORE *will be the realm of the kindness of God and the exceeding riches of His grace.*

The content, the intent, and extent of eternal life is to know God the Father and the Son through the eternal Spirit (Jn. 17:3). The successive ages then will be marked out by revelations of God to His own as He unfolds out of His infinite being, the everlasting burnings of His majesty and glory. There, in the midst, His saints shall dwell and know no fear. Wave after wave of the beneficence of God will bathe their redeemed souls with rapturous joy, providing glorious themes for songs and service, throughout the far extensions of His everlasting empires. FOREVERMORE *will be the realm of the knowledge and enjoyment of God.*

Wherever the child of God will be in those vast realms, the Lord will be. Wherever the Lord will be, there His own will dwell in safety by Him forever, for His Word is clear, "ever . . . with the Lord" (1 Thess. 4:17). FOREVERMORE *will be the realm of the visible presence of the Lord Himself.*

Is it any wonder then, that the Lord should conclude that unveiling of Himself with a glimpse into the ineffable glory of FOREVERMORE, with a grand "Amen." So every child of God, though bound for this while, like ancient Job, in a cage of ribs, can peer into the mists of the great forever and lift his voice and add his own "Amen."

"Timeless eternity, shoreless infinity, measureless, limitless, fathomless sea!
Final infixity, never to pass away, ever and ever and ever to be!

Life's perpetuity, Love's continuity, ceaseless and sinless, in fullness and free!
Joyous futurity, blessed security, ever and ever and ever to be!

Judgment's immensity, torment's intensity, fearful finality, changeless decree!
Conscious nonentity, sinful identity, ever and ever and ever to be!

Purpose immutable, kindness inscrutable, Christ for the sinner accursed on the tree!
Grace unaccountable, Love unsurmountable, ever and ever and ever to be!

Anguish or ecstasy, peace or perplexity, infinite, absolute, offered to thee!
Pause on the brink today, ponder eternity: ever and ever and ever to be!"

Emergency!

"I will never leave thee nor forsake thee."
                    (Heb. 13:5)

To smell and feel the cold and fetid breath
Of Death pursuing:
The plug of life pulled out
And strength is draining fast.
The tingling numbness creeps
Like the unrelenting tide, it sweeps
O'er fingers, hands and arms.
The long dark tunnel
Opens wide its gaping mouth ahead.

Red lights flashing on the monitor
Silent, swiftly moving figures, all in white
With steel tipped fingers
Opening up hot points for life to enter
Drip by drip, or sudden surge.
Quiet assuring voices
Asking questions
The brain can't seem to fit together
With an answer.

And it's then he comes,
Out of the corner where he's been lurking
All the day
Waiting for the weakening.
Yapping at the heels of the soul
Hyena-like, his howl awakens fear.
Circling, slavering, around
He mocks our feeble faith,
And scorns "Where now thy God?"

Where is that verse again?
The one we need right now,
Can't remember.
Where are those heavenly thoughts
We've read that others had
Here in the Valley?
Can't think!
Then pray—Pray now!
But cannot seem to put this unknown need
In any form of prayer.
Then rest! Ah, that's it—rest!
For Jesus, Lord, is here, and standing by,
Strong and knowing all,
Sure and unhurried.
There HE waits, though silently,
You cannot doubt it now,
He is there.

Loved ones stand around,
Eyes closed, silent moving lips
Put into prayer, our pressing needs.
The coward hound of hell
Has scurried off.
That strong, that Holy Presence
Was enough
To make him scrabble to his corner hole
Without a backward glance.
The heart cries of loved ones
Pierce the black, and do what we are too weak to do.
The thankful mist envelops.
This is all . . . HE IS HERE!
And so we nestle in the crook
Of that tender, mighty arm
And rest,
Rest,
Rest.

What's the Difference?

Perhaps it is the flood of new Bible translations, but there seems to have befallen us a general slackness in the handling of the holy Word of God. There is a carelessness in some areas with the quotation of Scripture. Perhaps because newer translations, in general, lack the cadence and euphony of the old KJV, there is less habitual memorizing of Scripture today. Memorizing some modern translations, of course, is not easy. It is like trying to memorize a column in the newspaper, with its flat, lackluster vocabulary.

But this is not about translations, we all have our favourites, it is about the careless attitude to the holy Scriptures that ignores its beautiful accuracy and fails to distinguish things that differ. For example, Daniel was not thrown into the lions' den, as some would say. He was thrown into "the den of lions." What's the difference? The lions! A fairly significant difference to Daniel that day!

Noah and the ark have been fodder for the pseudo-intellectuals who, having calculated the cubic capacity of the vessel, mock the record, claiming that there wasn't enough room in the ark for everyone to be saved. Then they blame God for being dishonest. What's the difference? These critics do not understand that the ark wasn't built to save the people IN the flood. It was built to save the world *from* the flood, if they would repent in time. It is not the sailing of the ark that is emphasized in Scripture, but the "preparing" of it. Every plank was a sermon, every hammer blow a warning, and as the structure grew, so did the responsibility of the viewers. The ark was not built by Noah to save the population, but "to the saving of his house," after the world rejected his preaching (Heb. 11:7). Now these may or may not be significant examples, but as this attitude to the Word of God becomes prevalent, we begin to see and hear some alarming aberrations that can affect the corporate and individual testimony of the believers.

It is incumbent upon us all to "rightly divide the Word of truth" and thereby be not ashamed (2 Tim. 2:15). We must maintain the distinctions God has made between the old covenant and the new, Israel and the Church, the believer's state and the believer's standing, the Lord's Table and the Lord's Supper, the baptism of the Spirit and the filling of the Spirit, and so on.

Failure to do so leads to confusion, if not indeed into outright error. For instance, any move, as under the old covenant, to establish again a special caste of priests or ministers, with special titles, some even wearing special garments, ministering before man-made altars in earthly sanctuaries, is not progress at all, but a great step backwards. It is an endeavour to resurrect what God has laid to rest and to promote what Christ has finished. It is to divide an equal brotherhood into an unscriptural "clergy" and "laity," which thing, we read, the Lord hates (Rev. 2:15).

Failure to recognize the difference between man-made regulations and the Word of God has led, in some places, to a sectarian spirit which receives into fellowship those who conform to the rules and rejects those who, for conscience sake, cannot. Thus it is possible that a carnal believer who keeps the man-made rules may be received, while a spiritual one who doesn't may be refused—a solemn responsibility to face at the Bema.

The difference between the temple worship with its service under the old covenant, and the ministry of New Testament believers in the Church is clearly not understood by some. In a recent book on the ministry of women, the author calls up Old Testament examples to substantiate his ideas for what womens' participation in the service of the local church should be. What confusion! How we thank the Lord for godly women and the special influence they have in the churches—where would we be without this?—but it is clear that there are differences between the old order and the local church ministries in the New Testament.

Perhaps one of the most urgent needs in the church today is for men of discernment. Men who can sense the approach of error, and have the uncommon courage to do something about it. Men who can clearly distinguish between things that differ and not be influenced by those who seemingly can't tell the difference between soul and spirit, the world and the Word, happiness and holiness, quantity and quality, the cemetery and the sanctuary.

O Book of wondrous depths and heights, and glories ever new,
Which in ten thousand various lights, brings Jesus into view.
O, who would leave the Fountainhead to drink the muddy stream,
Where man has mixed what God hath said with every dreamer's dream.

Dear Dokimos

I n the constant search for helpful written ministry that would be suitable to include in *Counsel* magazine, the editor frequently finds himself leafing through the brittle pages of some very old publications. The writers of those aging documents are all in the glory and they rest from their labours. They little thought that, in some distant land and far-off day, a man like me would read their yellowed page and draw sustenance from what they penned with ink-dipped quill in the dim light of an oil lamp, or sputtering candle.

Such thoughts led me on to wonder who at last may read these words taken from an issue of *Counsel* magazine. Perhaps, after the Church has been caught up to glory, a tribulation saint, in some attic refuge has just discovered this very copy among bundles of old papers. With trembling hand and furtive glance, he turns the pages, and wonders who were those writers, whose names appear in the index? How did they live for God in their day? What was the condition of the Church before they were so suddenly caught up from the earth to glory? Does that dear suffering saint not deserve an honest answer? Will an open letter suffice?

Dear Tribulation Saint, Dokimos,

Greetings in the Name of Christ Jesus, our Lord and yours. We have gone to glory and anticipate your soon deliverance. Let us at once affirm that our beloved Lord Jesus is more radiantly glorious than ever we imagined, even in our highest and holiest moments on earth. All heaven is illumined by the shadowless light of the Lamb, a glory that excels the spectrum of the rainbow. The atmosphere is sweet and fresh with the fragrance of the Lily. The armies of heaven are assembling, soon to follow the King of kings and Lord of lords in battle array.

Take heart, beloved of the Lord, your suffering will soon be over and He will come whose right it is to reign, and the glory of the Lord will cover the earth as the waters cover the sea. You wonder who we were, how we lived and what was the condition of the Church while we waited for the Lord from Heaven?

Of course, we were only sinners saved by matchless grace and redeemed by the precious blood of Christ. In those pre-rapture days we were rich and increased with learned expositions. We grew fat on theological dainties while we 'dialogued' about social problems and religious questions that cost us absolutely nothing. We feasted on our own fellowships and separated ourselves from other saints who did not agree with our man-made rules and regulations. We built magnificent meeting places and fed one another there with the finest of Biblical instruction and religious entertainment.

We stepped up the cadence of our music and turned up the volume to attract the world. We did not seem to hear the sob of the sorrowing, the cry of the brokenhearted and the wail of perishing souls. We tapped our toes to the world's tunes and got involved in the world's politics. The final fury of which, you, dear fellow believer, are suffering now.

We worshipped our idols in the domed temples of sport and, as fan-atics, we sacrificed countless hours we could never recall. We zipped up our Bibles in plastic Bible bags on Sunday evenings and unzipped them again the next Sunday morning. We preached orderly, eloquent, fervent sermons on Sundays, then subjected our families and workmates to our ill temper on Mondays. This, because Christ was replete in our homiletics but not reigning in our hearts or homes.

We relegated precious truths of the Church to our library shelves to gather dust and replaced them with carnal alternatives and the organized methods of big business. We discarded the God-given symbol of submission, called it culture only for Corinth, irrelevant for our day, and caused obedient angels to wonder in silence at such an insult to their glorious Lord, and gave the rebellious angels opportunity to gloat that, at last, a creature glory was displayed in the Church.

We formed religious corporations with self-appointed offices to control millions of money, which we invested in the stocks and bonds of the world's system to get still more money. All the while, overwrought missionaries struggled with broken printing presses and woefully inadequate equipment. Missionary hospitals and clinics lacked modern facilities and adequate stocks of medical supplies.

Outside the door of our complacency, malnourished children with distended stomachs gazed in silence, and far-off multitudes hungered for bread and died, drugged in the dark. Worn-out missionary vehicles, loosened and rattled by jungle roads and washboard trails, lay silently rusting, waiting for tires, batteries and

spare parts. Aged believers in our own towns, urgently needing nursing care and comfort in a Christian atmosphere, had to leave their loved ones and their familiar places, to find a distant haven, or else go to the world's provision for a place to end their days.

Men—and women—rose up and sought to turn God's people aside from the truth, diverting them away from the Lord Jesus with religious forms and innovations. Some even turned backwards to childish things, seeking signs and wonders and became preoccupied with subjective experience. Others, charged with the care of the flock of God, became so busy in the world and their own affairs, that they hired a man to do their work, and left him to it.

The gospel of the glory of the blessed God was rarely heard in its purity and power. In many places the gospel meeting was discarded as "outdated," or we replaced it with yet another introverted fellowship meeting. Meanwhile, lost men and women drove past our beautiful buildings, and wondered what was going on inside.

Yet in spite of our lukewarm condition, the Lord did not forsake us. He knocked and knocked and knocked again, ever seeking an entrance, to take His rightful place within. Thankfully, here and there, there were individuals, and repentant companies of God's people who heard His voice and opened up to enjoy His rich provision. These lived holily, loved greatly, served faithfully, and looked earnestly for the Lord to come, and they finished well.

Dear tribulation saint, we cannot wish for your suffering, but perhaps had we known more about persecution than profits, more about pain than the world's pleasures, more separation from it and its methods than wallowing in them, this letter would have been different and our reward also. We did hear a distant, muffled cry at times, but we were so comfortable in our upholstered pews, it disturbed us only slightly. It went something like this, "Awake thou that sleepest and arise from among the dead . . . ." Then, one ordinary day, the Lord Jesus came and took us by surprise to glory. So ended for us, life's mortal day on earth.

Still you remain, to glorify God in your body and in your spirit by life or by death. Faint not, beloved; soon the King in His glory and beauty will appear for you. Be thou faithful unto death. Your crown awaits. So that you, and by His grace, even we also, shall be to the praise of His glory. Until then, farewell, beloved sufferer, faithful servant, weeping singer. Soon God shall wipe away the tears of sorrow from your eyes, as He has already wiped the tears of remorse from ours.

Dokimos, always signifies "approved." It is translated in James 1:12 by the phrase "when he is tried" (or tested). The word is used of coins and metals in the Septuagint. In Zechariah 11:13, in regard to the 30 pieces of silver, we read, "Cast them into a furnace and I will see if it is good (approved) metal."
—from W. E. Vine's *Expository Dictionary of New Testament Words*

God is Good . . . But!

What was that again? "But"? Whoever would say such a thing? Well, the man who said it was a "seer", a prophet and a chief man, holding a most responsible position in the sacrificial ministry of the praise of God. Asaph was one of the 38,000 Levites set apart for the ministry of the holy things. The Levites were divided into four groups: 24,000 were responsible to "set forward the work of the house of the Lord"; 6,000 were officers and judges; 4,000 were "porters." That leaves four thousand. Those were the musicians. Out of those were selected 288 choristers, "instructed in the songs of the Lord." They were divided into 24 small groups, or "courses," 12 in each. Each course had a leader, and over the combined choir was the "chief musician." That was Asaph.

Now if we were going to select a chief musician for the praise of God in Israel, what skills would we expect? Some played on the harp, some on the psaltery, but we read of Asaph that his expertise was that "he made a sound with the cymbals—CRASH!" Now, to a non-musician, as is this writer, that would hardly seem like a lot of talent. In fact, to the untrained observer, Asaph's gift may not have appeared as brilliant as the harpist running his skilled fingers over the strings. Appearances can be a problem. For this banger of cymbals was indeed the "chief" musician, a seer who "prophesied according to the order of the king."

I discovered also from a musician that there is more to playing the cymbals than just a great "sound" now and again. The vital thing is timing. A great enthusiastic crash of cymbals at the wrong time would be disastrous. Yet it is in those very areas of appearances and timing that Asaph ran into difficulty. He wrote twelve psalms: Psalm 50, and Psalms 73-83. It is in the 73rd Psalm he bares his soul.

As a Levite he was separated to the Lord and "lived by faith" from the free-will offerings of the people. He ran into severe difficulties when he got his eyes off the Lord and was distracted by "the prosperity of the wicked" (v. 3). That great "but" in verse 2 echoes serious doubts. He had no doubts as to the goodness of God, "but" he himself was the problem. His faith was assailed by a deep perplexity and he was tempted through those age old avenues, "the lust of the eye," "the lust of the flesh" and "the pride of life." As a servant of the Lord living by faith, he saw the prosperity of the ungodly, the suffering of the godly and was perplexed by the silence of God. He was not the first to be so distressed, and he wasn't the last either.

He saw and envied the success of the wicked. They prospered. He seemed to envy the excess of the wicked in their luxurious life-style, and he wondered at the process of their lives, fat and faithless, prosperous and proud, corrupt and careless. Yet they lived on . . . and on . . . and on. They seemed to have no problems of disease, no retribution on their defilement and when they came to die they just slept away.

When he looked at himself and his limited means, and the humbling experience of living by the gifts of others, he was tempted to think wrong thoughts of God on the basis of how things *appear* to be (v. 13). He was tempted to speak wrong things about God and blame Him for the problem (v. 15). He was tempted to give no thanks to God and take his adequate daily blessings for granted (v. 14). He felt "chastened every morning" and forgot that the Lord's compassions were new every morning.

However, this banger of cymbals knew "there is a time to keep silent," so he exercised the discipline of silence. He considered the consequences of his words on others (v. 15). He had forgotten for a moment that *we do not live unto ourselves.* He exercised the discipline of submission. He considered the consequences of worldliness on the lives of others (v. 10). He had forgotten that *we cannot live as we please.* Then he exercised the discipline of the sanctuary. He considered the consequences in his own life if he should live without it: slipping feet, a saddened heart, and a suffering conscience. *He learned that we do not live as we should.* There, in the silence of the sanctuary, Asaph saw the wicked again, but from God's perspective and eternity's view. "Then saw I their *end*." Ah! that's it. "What will ye do in the end thereof!" asks Jeremiah. It is the end that counts.

The world envies the life-styles of the "rich and famous" and chases uncertain riches. The worldling appears to have more leisure, more luxury, more laughter than the earnest believer. There are battles they will never fight. They know nothing of earnest confession of sin and daily washing in the presence of God. They are ignorant of the tests of faith, of the Father's rod, the Husbandman's blade and the labourer's yoke.

"But . . ." Yes there is another "but." If they remain in their sins, they will perish. Let us not envy the wicked. This is their only heaven. Let us weep for them in the secret place and with the fragrance of the sanctuary upon us go out to tell them of their only hope of salvation, the God who is good, not only to Israel, but to all them that call upon Him in faith in His beloved Son. Then their last end will be like the righteous.

The Wasted Years

There are some noble souls who have no regrets. Faithful, godly, and undeviating in their love and loyalty to Christ, the beauty of their walk and the evident power of their words give evidence of lives of unswerving devotion. Then there are others of us who could sing the old hymn:

"O the years in sinning wasted, could I but recall them now,
I would give them to my Saviour, to His will I'd gladly bow."

They began with zeal. With the stub of a sword they would have faced an army for the Lord Jesus. Fearlessly they engaged the enemy. They threw themselves into the fray, and distinguished themselves in battle for God and for His gospel. Then something happened. Perhaps a tragic fall. Perhaps a slow disintegration, a growing dullness permitted to the things of God. Perhaps increased excursions into the world, or yielding to the merciless claims of business. Prayer and the Word were gradually eclipsed and a comfortable sleepiness fell on the soul. The frost silently settled on the heart and the fruit withered on the vine.

The gentle breezes of love and grace wafted across that soul from time to time, and awakened it to a sweet fellowship, an inspiring message, a word in season, or one of the songs of Zion. The eyes of the heart were lifted up to look again longingly to heaven. But the enemy, cruel and merciless as ever, crushed every hope of recovery, "Too late!" he cried. With a sad lament the heart again bowed downward to the dust and inward to its own despair.

Dear reader, is this your case or the condition of a friend you long to see arise again? Faint not! There is hope! Not in any seminar or novel program, but in the sure knowledge that God is a God of recovery, who delights to restore the repentant soul, and turn His anger away (Hos. 14:4).

In 2 Kings 8, Gehazi was recounting to the king "all the great things Elisha had done." Among these mighty works was the report of how the prophet had restored a dead son to his mother. Then a remarkable thing happened! Some would call it "coincidence," but we know better. "*As*" Gehazi was telling of this amazing incident, the very woman in the report is brought before the king. Gehazi, with astonishment exclaims, "O king, this is the woman, and this is her son." She had gone to Philistia because of the famine. The government had taken over the land on which to grow crops. Now she has returned to beg for her property to be returned.

The king's response is most instructive. He appointed an officer with this command, "Restore all that was hers, and all the fruit of the field since the day that she left the land, even until now."

There is a wonderful promise of God to His people, "I will restore to you the years that the locust hath eaten" (Joel 2:25). The king's word is a picture of a grander work of God. This is the restoration of the *fruit* of the wasted years. If an earthly king can do that for one of his impoverished subjects, then our God is able to do even more wonderfully.

Jonah was the only sign the Lord Jesus gave the scribes and Pharisees of His death and resurrection. Yet Jonah was fleeing from the will of God in disobedience. Then when he acknowledged that his was the fault, he was carried beneath the waves and brought out again to be a sign of the Saviour's deep sufferings, death and resurrection. Yet another case where sin abounded, grace did much more abound, for "a greater than Jonah is here."

Would you or I have included Samson in the list of the mighty in faith of Hebrews 11? Yet, from his blinding, binding, grinding prison, he lifted his sightless eyes to heaven and cried, "O Lord . . . only this once"—and the record shows that those he slew in his death were more than those he slew in his life and his name is recorded in Hebrews 11. This is not an excuse for slothful or careless living, taking advantage of the grace of God—"God forbid"—but it is a ray of hope for those who have given up, thinking it is too late for them now and they have settled down to a life of distant mediocrity and a sometime spirituality.

There are gifted men, who once felt the call of God to missions, or to some special service, but never responded. Now retired, and accepting failure as a fact of life, they try to fill their days in some sunny waiting room for heaven. Still there are fields of evening labour. There is no prize for early quitters in the Bible, but there is a prize even for the late starters (Mt. 20:9). There are assemblies in Africa, India, the Orient, where English is understood and the saints are hungering for the spiritual food that perhaps the reader could impart. Wasted years? Let it not end that way. Our God can restore the fruit even of those years and "at evening time it shall be light."

Remember Them

"Remember them that have gone before"
Hebrews 13:7 (transl.)

Remember them!
They are a dying breed.
Softness and comfort they never sought,
But onward through the trackless night
And blistering day they went;
Carving a path untrod before
To reach some wandering soul,
Even one,
Remember them!

Remember them!
With tent and heavy bag,
And food for the day, and little else,
But ever an eye to their Heavenly Father
Whom they trusted for their needs
Begging from no man,
And in simple faith
They walked with God,
Remember them!

Remember them!
And help-meets left at home,
Eking out their little day by day
In loneliness and mighty prayers
Following their loved partner
As he searched for lost and perishing
Who cared little for his tears and toil
And urgent call.
Remember them!

Remember them!
When lounging at thine ease,
Or pressured by this world's bold claim
Or filling up thy time in idle sport,
Grumbling at failing saints perhaps
Remember them! Their Master does,
And on that day of Great Review
They'll shine, and hear the grand "Well done."
Remember them!
Yes, Remember them
And thank your God
That ever one of these nobility
Passed your way
And touched your life.

Is There Anyone in Charge?

National calamities, tragedies on land and sea and in the air have shocked us. Governments cry "Peace, peace" while social unrest erupts in violence. Thousands of dollars are spent, and nations co-operate with ships and helicopters, to save a few icebound whales from dying, while unborn babies are aborted every day, thrown into garbage bags and reduced to a handful of ashes in the basements of government registered clinics.

Officers of the law are frustrated, as criminals laugh their way out of court, released on some legal technicality. Rapists and murderers walk the streets on weekend passes and early paroles, while fearful law-abiding citizens line up at the hardware counters, to buy security devices to bar themselves in their own homes.

Standards plunge and goodness, honesty and purity become fodder for the world's ungodly comedians. The Holy Name of God erupts in blasphemy from the lips, even of children. Values are utterly confused. Sports idols are awarded multi-million dollar contracts, while dedicated nurses, serving under high stress and saving human lives, are paid barely a living wage.

Is there anyone in charge? Is there somewhere a master plan? Or is the whole complicated system of things just running down and out of control?

Thankfully, we can turn to the Word of God to find the answer. In Daniel 9:24, we read, "I am the Lord which exercise lovingkindness, judgment, and righteousness in the earth: for in these things I delight."

God governs in the material, moral, and spiritual realms, according to specific laws. In the material realm He governs by natural laws. He governed its design as Creator, He governs its daily existence as Sustainer, and its destiny as the Sovereign. There is no mercy in the laws of nature. Break them and there is instant retribution. Every electrician knows that!

In the moral realm, God governs by providential laws. If these are followed, mankind is benefited. If man chooses his own way, then he will reap the bitter harvest of his violation. Public unrest, ecological imbalance, social diseases, broken homes, broken hearts, broken lives, are all evidences that God's laws have been violated. Sadly, man's self-will causes the innocent to suffer with the guilty. Then, to add insult to injury, he shakes his fist to heaven and blames God for his misfortune!

However, there is some mercy in the providential laws of God. We discover in the Scriptures that if a nation, because of its national sins, comes under the hand of God for judgment, and there is true repentance, He will spare that nation for a while (Jer. 18:7-10).

We are living now in the age of God's grace. He does not instantly punish the sinner. Instead, because of the work of the Lord Jesus at Calvary, He extends His unmerited favour to all. So, for the present, He is dealing with a world of individuals whom He loves. He is calling them by His gospel to come to Him by faith.

God has infinitely better blessings in view, however, than a temporary "health, wealth and happiness." These are eternal life and the unfading riches of a spiritual inheritance, consummated in glory where there is the fulness of joy, no pain, no sorrow, no tears and no death, (Eph. 1:3; Rev. 21:4).

In the spiritual realm, God's government is seen in His Church. Not man's "churches." He leaves them to their own confusion and the pomposity of their own prelates, priests, and self-appointed preachers. His Church, the Body of Christ, composed of every true believer in the Lord Jesus, has only one Head and He is in Heaven, not anywhere on earth (Eph. 1:20-23). His government is first direct, flowing from the Head, even Christ Himself, for development and discipline. Secondly, it is delegated, not through one man, however gifted and wonderful he may seem. It is through a plurality of elders in every scriptural assembly of the Lord's people. These shepherds are not elected nor appointed to a position by men, but made by the Holy Spirit to love, sacrificially serve, and guard the flock of God where they are (Acts 20:28). The Lord Jesus, said, "I will build My Church; and the gates of hell shall not prevail against it" (Mt. 16:18).

In spite of distress in the world, decay in society, and departure in the Church, above it all, we can be assured there is *God* controlling.

> We search the starlit Milky Way, a million worlds in rhythmic sway,
> Yet in our blindness some will say, "There is no God controlling!"
> But as I grope from sphere to sphere, new wonders crowd the eye, the ear,
> And faith grows firmer every year: "My God is there, controlling!" —W.W. Reid

# How Much?

"We esteemed Him not." Luther translates those words, "We esteemed Him as nothing." Our estimate of Christ is the crucial thing. Great thoughts of Christ make great Christians and little thoughts of Him make petty Christians whose values are inverted and whose vision is introverted. A number have left their estimates of Christ on record for our instruction— and warning.

There was *the crowd*. They estimated the value of Jesus against Barabbas. They said, "Give us Barabbas." They esteemed His value at less than that of a murderer. In grace, He pled their ignorance on the cross.

Herod and his "men of war." (What irony!) They left their estimate of Christ on record, "they set Him at nought." If only they had known who He was that they crowned with thorns, anointed with spittle, and beat with fists! Could they have but seen the serried ranks of His heavenly host standing at attention, waiting for His single command, they might have died in shock!

The religious hierarchy have left their estimate of Christ on record: "They covenanted with (Judas) for thirty pieces of silver." They knew, and Judas knew, the law of values (Lev. 27). The "estimation" of a male between the ages of twenty and sixty was 50 shekels. If it be a female, 30 shekels. Not that the woman servant was intrinsically of lesser value, certainly not, but by reason of her child-bearing and rearing, her services would be thereby limited. So the priests mockingly covenanted for the price of a woman servant.

What is the estimate of *the Lord* Himself in the day of His sorrow? Seldom does man properly evaluate himself. Either he will overrate himself in pride, or undervalue himself in humility. In Psalm 22:6, through the mouth of the Psalmist, He cries out, "I am a worm and no man." He was taking our place. Though sinless and spotless, "He was made in the likeness of sinful flesh." The Lord had said to the patriarch, "I will help thee, thou worm Jacob." Bildad said, "man, which is a worm." We just cannot say it, but He did, prophetically, "I am a worm" as He took our place in the dust.

What is the estimate of *the Father*? Ah! this is right! "He raised Him from the dead, and set Him at His own right hand in the heavenly places, Far above all . . ." His exalted place in glory reveals the estimate and delight of the Father.

What do *the saints in heaven* think of Him? What is their estimate? John was permitted to discover this and to record it, "And I beheld, and I heard the voice of many angels round about the throne and the beasts and the elders: and the number of them was ten thousand times ten thousand, and thousands of thousands; saying with a loud voice, Worthy is the Lamb that was slain to receive power and riches, and wisdom, and strength, and honour, and glory, and blessing. And every creature which is in heaven, and on the earth, and such as are in the sea, and all that are in them, heard I saying, Blessing, and honour, and glory, and power, be unto Him that sitteth upon the throne, and unto the Lamb for ever and ever. And the four beasts said, Amen. The four and twenty elders fell down and worshipped Him that liveth forever and ever" (Rev. 5:11-14).

To this great estimate of Christ, as the worthy Lamb, every believer can add his own "Amen." Before this vision of His worth and glory every believer will fall down and render holy worship.

But what is our estimate of Him here and now? We know by His unfailing promise that when we gather together in His Name, He actually is there. We so often sense His real presence as we take the bread and wine at the Lord's Supper. We sing:

> *"Amidst us our Beloved stands*
> *And bids us view His pierced hands,*
> *Points to His wounded feet and side,*
> *Blest emblems of the crucified."* (C. H. Spurgeon)

His promise is true also in the gospel meeting and in the prayer meeting, when we gather in His Name. What is my estimate then? Do I consider some other *thing* of more value than spending a brief hour with Him in the gathering of the saints? Is the meeting of the assembly an "it," or is it "Himself" to whom we gather?

If we could honestly advertise that the Lord Jesus would be visibly present in our next prayer meeting, the police would not be able to control the crowds. He *will* be there, but only "to faith's opened eye." Certainly legal duties press upon us and at times weakness prevents us, but when we are able to gather "unto Him," what could we tell Him is of greater value to us than He is?

Caught Up

"**D**o you think we'll ever get caught up?"

We were standing in the press room as brother Tim asked the question. The heady aroma of printer's ink, coated stock, and cleaning fluid filled the place. The measured rhythm of the presses, punctuated now and again with the soft crunch of the paper cutter, enthusiastically supported by the speedy clacking of the folder in the background all blended into a kind of mechanical malaria that old printers never quite get out of their system.

"Caught up"? Deadlines, of course were what it was all about. Those ever-present and pressing deadlines that seem to move over us in the night while we sleep (briefly). They are a lot like the dandelions in our garden. Get one dealt with and two more will replace them by the morning.

Yes, we will be "caught up." Nothing more sure, except that we cannot say just when that will be. Not only "caught up" with all the deadlines, but for the believer in Christ, it will be "caught up" and away from the realm of all that speaks of the dead. It is not a deadline for the Christian, but the lifeline of our hope, reaching within the veil where the Captain of our salvation has already entered and is the guarantee that . . .

"He'll not be in Heaven and leave me behind."

Yet, in a most solemn and searching way, the coming again of the Lord Jesus Christ for His Church, to catch them up to His own presence (the word *"rapture"* means just that), is a deadline every unbeliever might well fear. Think of a world without a single praying mother, or godly father, Christ-loving wife or husband! Often mocked and despised, the butt of the world's jesters, those "born-agains" will be gone, never to distress society again with their pronouncements of coming judgment, the declarations of "John 3:16," and many other words of life. The lovers of this world will be unhindered then in their Christless "New Age" to look downward, as they ever do, to their ancient god, "mother earth," worshiping and serving the creature rather than the Creator (Rom. 1:25).

The call to the lovers of God, especially in these days, is not to look down to this realm of graves and groans and granite stones, where the life story of loved ones, neighbors, and friends is frequently edited down to a few lines chiselled on a gravestone between the date of birth and death. So often it is with the plaintive postscript, "Rest in Peace" or, to sound a bit more religious, "Requiescat, in pace," or still more brief, befitting the speed of this life, just "R.I.P."

The believer in Christ has a higher focus, a heavenly destiny, a holy future, and a real peace in which to rest in the presence of the Lord forever. It is not surprising, then, that we are reminded in Scripture that ". . . *our citizenship is in Heaven; from whence also we look for the Saviour, the Lord Jesus Christ*" (Phil. 3:20).

As dark violence tears at society, as evil and corruption abound in high places, as an overloaded justice system makes deals with the guilty to relieve the glutted prisons, as idols of the masses are discovered at the last to have feet of clay, yet are applauded as their empty lifestyles are promoted to our youth, as governments totter and leaders fumble in their darkness for any gleam of hope, as all these forces converge upon the end of this millennium, how wonderful it is for the child of God to know that this may truly be "the year of our Lord," the year of His coming, when we shall at last be "caught up"! This is the hope of every believer in Christ and His Word.

When hope fades, the heart is sick, for *"Hope deferred makes the heart sick"* (Prov. 13:12). When hope fades, the soul is distressed. The psalmist cried, *"Why art thou cast down, O my soul? And why art thou disquieted in me? Hope thou in God"* (Ps. 42:5). When hope fades, the life is unhappy. Paul declared, *"If in this life only we have hope in Christ, we are of all men most miserable"* (1 Cor. 15:19). But there is glory in the graveyard, there is triumph over the tomb, there is singing in the sepulcher, for "Jesus is coming again!" This is our glorious hope, a sure hope, based—not on some dreamer's dream, some poet's pentameter, some theologian's theory—but on the living Word of the risen Lord. "We . . . shall be caught up" (1 Thess. 4:17).

Oh, joy, oh, delight, should we go without dying!
No sickness, no sadness, no dread, and no crying!
Caught up through the clouds with our Lord into glory,
When Jesus receives His own.
O Lord Jesus, how long? . . . —H. L. Turner

Follow Me

The San Luis Valley snuggles at the foot of the Sangre de Cristo Mountains in Colorado. These drain the clouds before they can refresh the valley which has one of the lowest rainfalls in the U.S. Powerful winds whip sand from the desert on the east through a narrow defile into the valley and form great dunes where people have been lost. However, the valley is watered by irrigation from the Rio Grande River and the farmers there grow some of the finest alfalfa available anywhere for dairy cattle.

The first time I went there, I stayed at John's place. This brother at that time had the care of 2000 sheep and 1200 baby lambs! One day I was taken to the fold containing the ewes and their offspring. As I endeavoured to walk through to the far side, the sheep struggled to get away from me. I was a stranger and not known to the sheep.

A little while later, the shepherd came to the fold. He was every inch a character from the Old West. A battered Stetson shielded his eyes. His weathered face told of years spent in the open air and the bowing of his blue jeans witnessed to long years in the saddle. He made his way over to where I was standing, but he had to knee his way through. The sheep didn't even lift their heads. They knew him, you see.

He told of summer days when the flock would be taken to the foothills to pasture. There he would live with them till the end of the summer. Feeling at one time he had shepherded long enough, he wanted to pass the work on to a younger man. But shepherds are scarce. At last one young man claimed the job, and he was taken to the flock, and a cabin on the mountainside.

The old shepherd, however, had not forgotten the sheep, and after a few days felt he should run out to see how things were going. The young man gave him a relieved welcome. The sheep were terribly restless. The shepherd just began to walk among them, speaking to them quietly. One by one they began to lie down until the whole flock was at rest. They knew his voice.

While we spoke, I noticed a little lamb over to the one side, all alone, shivering and bleating pathetically. "What's wrong with that little fellow?" I asked.

"Oh," replied the shepherd, "He's lost his mother."

Looking over the sea of gray wool and hundreds of (to me) identical sheep, I asked, "How will he ever find his mother now?"

He scanned the flock, and replied, pointing to one ewe, "There's his mother over there."

"Now," I asked in surprise, "How can you know that?" "Watch," was his curt response. In a moment or two, the mother sheep looked over at the trembling lamb and let out an authoritative bleat. The lamb didn't hesitate; it dashed over to its mother and snuggled into her wool. The mother turned her head around and gave the lamb a little bump, as much as to say, "Now, don't run away again."

I looked over that flock and couldn't help but ask again, "But among all those sheep, how did you know for sure which one was the mother?" It was almost a look of reproach he gave me as he glanced my way from under the old Stetson, "Mister, I know my sheep."

It was an answer right from Scripture (Jn. 10:14). The Lord Jesus said it first, and likely the old shepherd didn't realize he was speaking the same words as the Good Shepherd long ago.

What a comfort it is to remember that each believer is likened to a sheep and the Lord Jesus is the Good Shepherd. Stepping into the unknown pathway ahead may cause us to tremble. Until we hear the Good Shepherd speak again, "My sheep hear My voice, and I know them, and they follow Me" (Jn. 10:27).

We must pass through the sunrise to reach tomorrow, but not the Good Shepherd. He is beyond the sun. He inhabits eternity. He is already in all our tomorrows. He is up ahead, making sure the road is not too rough nor the path too steep for, "He will not suffer you to be tempted [tested] above that ye are able" (1 Cor. 10:13). He knows His sheep. Not just their identity—He knows them through and through: every drawing of the breath (Dan. 5:23), every tear of the eye (Ps. 56:8), every secret of the heart (Ps. 44:21).

As we, His sheep, step into the unknown pathway ahead, we follow our Shepherd. There are no surprises to Him. The lion, the wolf, the serpent are no match for Him. His rod and His staff assure our comfort, His mighty sacrifice secures our souls. We are in His hand (Jn. 10:28).

Who can tell, but perhaps it will be this year that we shall all be gathered together as one flock into one fold, never to go out again.

Loved

"As the Father hath loved Me so have I loved you" (Jn. 15:9).

"But, Lord I cannot feel Thee near,
I cannot pierce the gloom,
The voice of comfort, I can't hear
Within this lonely room.

O wilt Thou come from Thy far throne,
Beyond the thunder's roar,
And melt this heart, that feels like stone,
Draw near, draw near once more."

"Ah, child, why seek both far and wide
My Presence, wearily?
I never yet have left thy side,
Since thou first trusted Me."

"But, Lord, I want to feel Thy love
Caress this heart of pain;
Have I not sinned 'gainst Thee above?
Canst Thou love me again?"

"Ah, child, to me thou'rt ever dear
Where'er I see thy face;
If wandering far, in doubts, in fear,
Or in the Holy place.

Hast thou a friend who prays for thee?
Thou dost not doubt his care,
And yet he did not bleed for thee,
Thy sins he did not bear.

Ah, rest in this, I still love thee,
I cannot love thee more;
For as the Father loveth Me
My love on thee I pour."

Incredible!

There is a photograph of a grave in my files that is most unusual. The grave belongs to a German princess of a bygone day. She was an infidel and when she came to die she raised the final token of her infidelity against God—her last will and testament.

She left on record that her grave was to be covered with a great granite block. This was to be supported around by other blocks and all were to be chained together with heavy iron links. As a last rebellion, there was to be chiseled in the great block the words, "This grave is purchased to eternity and shall never be opened."

However, God does not need a resurrection to open a grave. As the body of this infidel was being lowered into its narrow bed, something else went in beside the coffin. From the tree that shaded the grave, gracefully and silently floated down a single seed. The body was buried, the grave was closed, and eventually the great stones sealed the body forever in the tomb.

"Forever" did I say? Well that was the wish of the ungodly woman who feared to be raised and to meet a holy God. No, the grave would not be sealed forever. The little seed that had been buried beside her body possessed something the wealthy princess had no longer—the germ of life.

Soon the seed germinated and began its relentless path toward the light, passing without hindrance between the linked stones that weighed upon the earth. Just a green slip it appeared to be, then a stalk, soon a sapling—and the irresistible power put into it by the princess's rejected God began to press the stones apart. Larger grew the tree and the links were stretched to the limit.

Whether in the black of night or at high noon we cannot tell when it happened. It would not surprise us a bit if it took place exactly on the day and the hour of the anniversary of that sad and hopeless funeral, but it happened no doubt with a violent crack. The chains snapped, the stones released, spread apart, and the tree still grew.

The old photograph I have shows the grave and the tree growing upward towards that place the tragic infidel will never see. As for the stones, not one of them is in its original position.

Still, the words can be clearly read carved in the stone, "This grave is purchased to eternity and shall never be opened." This opened grave is a solemn testimony to the truth of Galatians 6:7, "Be not deceived; God is not mocked: for whatsoever a man soweth, that shall he also reap."

Her grave will be opened yet again, but on that day she will obey the irresistible command to come forth. The Lord has declared it, "Marvel not at this: for the hour is coming, in the which all that are in the graves shall hear His voice" (Jn. 5:28). What a coming forth that will be!

The greatest miracle known to man is the raising of the dead. Paul, before Agrippa, asked the gathered company, "Why should it be thought a thing incredible with you, that God should raise the dead?" (Acts 26:8).

The heart of the issue was that the Jesus whom Paul served, had been crucified, but was now seated above, a living Saviour. Paul would witness to them of that great truth from his own experience. He had seen and heard the risen Christ.

The resurrection of Christ is *the basis of our faith*, "If Christ be not raised your faith is vain." Without this foundation, all preaching is empty, our witness is false, believing is groundless, forgiveness is meaningless, and trusting loved ones who have died have perished (1 Cor. 15:14-19).

That resurrection is *the basis of our hope*. For "if in this life only we have hope in Christ." then we have only misery as a companion and there is no hope beyond the grave. "But now is Christ risen from the dead" (1 Cor. 15:20). He is our hope.

That resurrection is *the basis of our love*. This is implicit in three words in 1 Corinthians 15. "Preaching" (v. 14). This suggests love to the saints, for their edification, exhortation, and comfort. "Witnesses" (v. 15) suggests love for the lost, in hopes that what has been learned of Christ will persuade men to likewise trust Him. "Testified" (v. 15) suggests love for the Lord as we stand for Him and for His cause in a hostile world.

No wonder we love to sing: "Hallelujah! Christ arose!"

Mighty stupendous power! Unique, triumphant hour!
Alive is He! Sure proof of righted wrong,
Earnest of ransomed throng, Spoils taken from the strong
Eternally!

70 Years in the Sanctuary

She was old and frail. Many years of domicile in the United States had not in the slightest taken the tartan edge off her broad Scottish accent. No longer able to attend the meetings of the Lord's people, she was lovingly cared for by her daughter and son-in-law. She sat in a rocker in a corner of the living room, back and forth, back and forth. However she was not idle. She was a woman of prayer. My colleague and I were engaged in a gospel series in the city where she lived and were considering bringing the series to an end on the next Lord's day, when we were invited for a meal and a visit with old Aunt Sarah.

She greeted us warmly with the comment, "I hope you boys are not going to stop these meetings yet"— well, we were planning to do just that on Lord's Day— ". . . and don't forget my brother Jimmy, I've prayed for him for *seventy years.*"

Uncle Jimmy was eighty, and lived only a few blocks away, so we decided we would drop over and see him and invite him out to the meetings. We were warned that he was "a wee hard-headed Scot," and if you know anything about that breed, you'll know they are not easily persuaded.

We found his place and knocked on the door. A fresh-faced, handsome gentleman opened it. His shining white hair enhanced his rosy cheeks. Short of stature, but evidently sprightly, he invited us in. He indicated where we should sit and he took his place in a well-worn chair that was positioned so that he could watch two different baseball games going on at the same time on two televisions! One in the bedroom and the other in the living room. He also had one going in the kitchen, in case he had to go to the fridge for a drink, he explained.

So there we were, trying to talk to this man about his never-dying soul, and all he could think about, it seemed, was baseball. At last, defeated, we left the old man to his preoccupation.

Next day we thought we should try again. So in the morning (hopefully before baseball) we knocked on his door. Noises indicated someone was there—he lived alone—but our Scottish friend didn't answer. Again defeated, we left.

"What are we going to do about Uncle Jimmy?" Another day, so much to do, an unlikely prospect and, we confessed, not much hope of a favourable response. Then we remembered the old prayer warrior. Rocking back and forth and pleading her case in the presence of God. We were ready to give up after a couple of days, and she had prayed for seventy years!

Ashamed of our lack of heart, we made our way again to the wee Scotsman's home. Our knock was quickly answered this time. It was almost as though we were expected. "Come in boys," he greeted us, with his fresh-faced smile. The welcome was so warm and generous, I wondered if it was a trap!

"Been thinking about you boys. I have a good story that you could use. Sit down." We sat. Then he regaled us with a long tale about a man getting on the wrong train.

"Uncle Jimmy," I said, when he finished, "Don't you see, you are the man in the story. You are the man on the wrong train!" He sat back in his chair, as though he had been hit.

"Uncle Jimmy," said my colleague, "Why don't you give up all your arguments and take Christ as your Saviour, and be saved?"

"You know boys, I think I'd better just do that," he said, and rising from his chair, he went over to an old sofa and got on his knees, we with him.

"O God," he cried out with emotion, "Forgive me of all my folly and save me from my sins." All the power of seventy years of praying landed on his head in five minutes and old Uncle Jimmy passed from death unto life. He lived for two more years to prove the reality of his salvation.

We bundled him into the car, drove him the six blocks to his old sister's house and shoved him in the door. What a sight! The old prayer warrior got out of her rocking chair and the two old-timers tottered across the room to embrace each other. "Oh, Jimmy, Jimmy," Aunt Sarah wept, "Ye're saved at last, I've prayed for you for seventy years." We wept for joy with them and laughed aloud at the grace and mercy of our God and the wonderful love that follows the sinner to the very end.

Well, they are both in the glory now. Beholding the face of the One they love. Those long seventy years of prayer on earth must seem now but the briefest moment from eternity's point of view.

Have you prayed long for that loved one? Faint not! God is "able to do exceeding abundantly above all that we ask or think, according to the power that worketh in us" (Eph. 3:20).

Why?

Deep behind the furrowed brow
And haunting eye,
Burns there, with fiercest flame
The question—"Why?"

Throbs within that aching breast;
As numb as wood,
A bleeding, broken heart,
Misunderstood?

The well of tears, long since dried up
Can't weep relief?
Nought but the hollow groan
Conveys thy grief?

Battled, storm tossed, almost crushed,
Can hardly pray?
And Scriptures, once well known
Seem far away?

Oh, where's the water that can quench
The raging fire
That man's injustice lights
In monstrous pyre?

God's justice, by man's unjust ways,
Is carried out:
And vast th' eternal plans pursued
In hours of doubt.

If, for one moment, we could see
With natural eye
The end result, 'twould surely hush
That question—"Why?"

If Only

There are few places we must go in life like a graveyard! Silent, dignified, still. The gardener does his best like the cosmetician to hide the horror of death and to conceal its corruption. But as we walk its perfectly formed paths, lined by much-too-tidy borders and view the ranks of granite stones, we are aware that this is not the rest of victory, it is the silence of defeat. Blow the trumpet over the grave if you will. Cover the casket with the flag if you must. Smother it all with a mountain of floral tributes and pronounce the eulogies. It is still defeat. For here deposited in crumbling caskets lie the bones of shattered hopes. Beneath this well-trimmed sod great plans lie buried in the hollow silent breasts of men who had no future left for their plans. Here in these narrow beds of dust lie dreams unfulfilled, joys untasted, service unfinished and debts unpaid.

We bid our last farewells and dry our tears to return to the lonely room to eat the bread of sorrow and drink the cup of weeping. At least that is how it would inevitably be but for a Voice, and what a voice! Speaking words, and what words! Words of hope and consolation, words of victory and rejoicing. The words of Jesus, the Son of God, *"I am the resurrection and the life: he that believeth in Me, though he were dead, yet shall he live: and whosoever liveth and believeth in Me shall never die. Believest thou this?"*

Lazarus was dead! His sisters had sent the word of the ailing brother to the Lord Jesus, but "He abode two days still in the same place where He was." What a paradox to those whom Jesus loved. The Great Physician did not seem to heed the call and death invaded the home in Bethany. For Lazarus it was too late. His sorrow was *the sorrow of failing resources* and his cry was seemingly unheard.

When at last the Lord Jesus came to Bethany, Martha went to meet Him. She becomes for us a picture of the Mind Groping for answers. Her sorrow was *the sorrow of faulty reasoning*. "If only Thou hadst been here my brother had not died." This was the problem of frustration. How many of God's suffering people have cried out "If only" things had been different this sorrow would not have happened. The people too added their voice to this reasoning. The problem was that they would have been satisfied with a lesser miracle. A sick Lazarus kept alive! The Lord had something much more wonderful in mind. How often we are satisfied with second best!

Strange as it may seem, the Lord in His sovereign wisdom even permits failure to happen. In this way we discover our utter helplessness and the glory of His love and power. Often we must see Him through our tears, that we might discover He is greater than our grief.

Mary's sorrow was different in a way. It was *the sorrow of a fearful reaction*. She "sat still in the house." She becomes for us a picture of the heart fainting. A sense of hopelessness causes Mary to withdraw in silence.

Some of the Lord's people react to the problem of unanswered prayer and seemingly hopeless grief by withdrawing from the fellowship of others, withdrawing from service, into silence. But to all such we may say, "The Master is come and calleth for thee." He has a miracle for you!

Lazarus was buried, bound and barred, a corpse, cold and corrupting. The Lord gave command to remove the stone. Why did He not do that Himself with His power? He was teaching His own a lesson on human responsibility. He will not do by a miracle what we can do by obedience.

Martha raised three objections. Lazarus was dead, it was too late! Dead four days, the condition had gone on too long! He stinketh, it was too bad! How often we object like this when the Lord wants to help us. Too late, Lord! Too long, Lord! Too bad, Lord!

The Lord teaches the mourners another lesson. The work He was about to do was not first life for Lazarus, nor joy for the bereaved. It was first for the glory of God!

Need a miracle? "Take ye away the stone!"

Looking off unto Jesus, my heart cannot fear,
Its trembling is still, when I see Jesus near;
I know that His power my safeguard will be,
For, "Why are you troubled?" He saith unto me.

The Great Distraction

Devilish devices, wicked wiles, impious invasions have all been weaponry in the army of hell to defile many a life, shatter many a soul and destroy the testimony of not a few of the Lord's beloved since Satan deceived and tempted our first parents. However, one of the secret weapons stockpiled in the armoury of this merciless and wicked enemy is most dangerous, and, sad to say, often successful.

Its effectiveness is, in part, due to its appealing design and also its clever camouflage. It is The Great Distraction. One thing the enemy does not want is for a believer to be occupied with Christ. Those people spell danger to the infernal strategy. They become worshippers of the Living God and of His glorious Son through the eternal Spirit. Satan hates worshippers, for they give to God His rightful portion in acceptable sacrifices. They are lovers of God, of His Word, of His people and of the lost for whom the Son of God died at Calvary, and they are mighty in prayer. These must be destroyed if possible or at the least, the credibility of their witness and testimony must be permanently wounded if the nefarious purposes of darkness are to succeed.

The wily strategist of the pit knows also that those Christ-centered lives will not be easily tempted by the disgusting and vile poisons of his ordinance. Indeed they will recoil from all such intrusion. Therefore he turns to his secret weapons department and selects The Great Distraction.

Of course, it is cleverly camouflaged and can appear as a number of things with which the believer is well acquainted and is, therefore, disarmed. "The cares of this life" (Mk. 4:19) can so preoccupy the mind and heart, that Christ is crowded out of His pre-eminence. That is just the ordinary stuff of life, which we can usually keep tidily sorted in the cupboards of the soul, until one thing piles on top of another and at last spills out and clutters the heart and mind with the mundane and the ordinary. Then the harried believer finds little time or taste for such heavenly occupation as the enjoyment of Christ in the soul. For the approach of that weapon we have a rather gentle word, it is called "worry."

"The deceitfulness of riches" is another arm of this devastating weapon. It approaches benignly at first as "honest ambition" to "get ahead" and "pay the bills." It seems so absolutely right, that any other attitude may be labelled as "sloth" "irresponsibility" or even downright "carelessness."

While there is clearly no sin in possessing riches, the danger comes when there is a subtle switch of control and the desire for money begins to possess the mind, command our concentration and dictate our actions, so that, what began as a permissible discipline, reveals its true colours eventually as "covetousness."

"The lusts of other things." Of all this wicked device, this is perhaps its most subtle aspect, "other things." This is what conquered the rich farmer in the Lord's parable—"good things" (Luke 12). That is their greatest danger, they can be "good" things. In fact Peter discovered on the mount that the Great Distraction can even be a holy thing. He had to discover in the shadowing cloud that even a holy "thing" is not Christ. He exulted in the light of that blazing countenance, "IT is good for US . . . ." The Father actually interrupted Peter's distracted rambling, "while he yet spake," to focus his attention on the only permissible obsession for the believer, "This is My Beloved Son, in whom I am well pleased; hear ye *Him*." In effect the Father was saying to Peter, "Don't talk—*listen*," and "Not *it*—*Him*."

So we see that we may be distracted by things, good things, even holy things. It may be a spiritual gift, a spiritual truth, a spiritual service, but if "it" becomes a self-serving pre-occupation of the mind and heart and does not lead to Christ, "IT" is nothing more than that—"IT." What Peter said may have been true, the "IT" was good for him, but no subjective experience, even on a holy mount, must be allowed to distract us from God's divine Centre.

The Great Preservative for this most subtle wile is found in the exhortation of the Word of God in Hebrews 3:1, "Consider the Apostle and High Priest of our confession, Christ Jesus." This concentration of the heart, mind and soul on the Person of the exalted Saviour in His anointed ministries, on our behalf, is the great preservative for the heart and its affection, the mind and its attention and the soul and its occupation.

"Consider" here, is a most powerful word. It is so much more than just a passive thinking about the Lord. It is translated "behold," as in Acts 7:31, when Moses "saw" the burning bush and "drew near to *behold*" why it was not consumed. That is considering the *why* of Christ. "Why did He love me so?" we sing. The response is wonder and worship.

It is translated "perceive," as in Luke 20:23, when the Lord Jesus "perceived" the meaning behind the spoken words. This is to consider the *what* of the words and ways of the Master. What He meant beyond His words, what He did beyond the visible deed, what His purpose was behind the act. The disciples learned this at the feet-washing (Jn. 13:12).

It is also translated "discover," as in Acts 27:39, when the storm-tossed mariners discovered a bay into which they drove the ship. They discovered the place first as their salvation. But then being saved, they discovered the name of the place, they discovered those who dwelt there, and no doubt many other beauties of their new abode.

This is to consider the *who* of Christ. To thrust our souls into spiritual explorations of the One who has become our salvation. The mountains of His majesty, the gardens of His fragrance and beauty, the vales of His sorrow and the rivers of His fullness are each and altogether glorious realms of discovery. There is no end to this commanded activity, for *"this is* life eternal, that they might know Thee, the only true God, and Jesus Christ, whom Thou hast sent" (Jn. 17:3). The pursuit of this Great Attraction is the INTENT of eternal life, the CONTENT of eternal life and the EXTENT of eternal life. There is nothing beyond this, though we range throughout His everlasting empires and penetrate the vanishing point of the ages of ages, "This *is* life eternal."

If we allow the enemy to distract us, we will lie down at last on the thorns of remorse, clutching to our cold hearts the "things" that seemed so important in the fever of life, "good things" perhaps, even some "holy thing," and learn, too late to alter or to mend our ways, that the Lord Jesus had been displaced from the throne of the life. Saved? Yes, still saved, but saved as by fire, with only the ashes of our *things* of wood, hay and stubble to leave at the feet of our Beloved.

> *Turn your eyes upon Jesus,*
> *Look full in His wonderful Face,*
> *And the things of earth will grow strangely dim,*
> *In the light of His glory and grace.* —H. H. Lemmel

There Is a Friend
(Proverbs 18:24)

When, in the midst of turmoil and confusion,
Crowds engulf the solitary thought,
When, 'spite the rushing multitudes profusion,
The heart is lone, a friend at hand is sought,
There is a Friend!

When there is laughter's music so beguiling
And all display the joy of pleasure's lot,
When, though the countenance is bright with smiling,
The heart is sad, a balm to heal is sought,
There is a Balm!

When it is night, and time for rest and sleeping,
All is still, by darkness deep enslaved,
When mem'ries bring forth tears in silent weeping,
The heart is tired, a rest from all is craved,
There is a Rest!

This is a Friend, who understands completely,
His the Balm that reaches where it pains,
And His the Rest, He's ministering so sweetly,
His heart of love, full sympathy contains,
O! What a Friend!

War!

The child of God faces formidable opposition in the daily pursuit of Christian living. Sometimes this antagonism to holy advance is blatant, outright, open attack. At other times, it invades by subtle infiltration. We become vulnerable when we do not recognize the direction from which the attack is coming and frequently do not identify the objective that the enemy is endeavouring to capture.

Sometimes the nature of human existence is considered to be the sum of feelings, intellect and will. The feelings are associated with the heart and its affections. The intellect is associated with the mind and its attention. The will is associated with the soul, the inner life and its occupation. Against these three citadels on the battlements of our personality there is an ongoing siege and frequent attacks of various intensity.

Against the feelings of the heart and its affections rises up *a place*. Yet it is more than just place. It is a place governed by a system. Often camouflaged by external beauty and glittering glories it can be most appealing. Its voice can be muted and like a symphony to the sensitive or pulsating and exciting to the sanguine. It is "the world", adaptable, ingenious, inventive and eminently subtle in its highly organized and persistent campaign to capture the heart and its affections.

The command is passed on to us from the Captain of our salvation, "Love not the world, neither the things that are in the world" (1 Jn. 2:15). To preserve the heart, *another place is* brought before us. "Let not your heart be troubled: ye believe in God, believe also in Me. In My Father's house are many mansions; if it were not so, I would have told you. I go to prepare a place for you" (Jn. 14:1-2). Yet again it is more than a locality. It includes a vast and glorious system of "things" (human language recognizes its limitation to describe them). So we are ordered to set our affection on things above, not on things on the earth (Col. 3:2). The far extensions of heavenly dominion, the soaring altitudes of heavenly majesty, the sights and sounds of heavenly wonder are made substantial only by faith (Heb. 11:1), but they are the eternal reality that eclipses the temporal and the transient.

Against the mind and its attention rises *a power*, insidious, insubordinate and entrenched. It is *the flesh*. Unlike the frontal attack of the world, the flesh is the secret service of the enemy, the fifth column within, the ever present traitor. It works silently, surreptitiously, and subtly, ever deploying its forces towards the control of the communications center, the mind. If the mind can be captured the whole person will be brought under control. For as a man thinketh . . . so is he (Prov. 23:7).

This power infiltrates by way of the portals of our personality, the members. It operates by using an intricate system already within, the law of sin which is in our members (Rom. 7:23). How then can we deal with this evil force? There is the Divine provision of *another power*, the indwelling Holy Spirit. We are no match for the flesh by ourselves, but the Spirit wars against the flesh and as we are subject to His direction and appropriate His power we gain a victory over it. Nevertheless it will not be until the final reveille that we shall be forever free of attack from this power (Rom. 7:25; Gal. 5:16-18).

Against the will and its occupation in the realm of the soul comes the fiercest antagonist of all, *a person*, the devil himself. Having used the distraction of the world and diversion by the flesh, now the enemy by deception, calls for unilateral action by the will in disobedience. Before the act of sin in the body there is the fact of sin in the will.

Thus the enemy seeks a place of occupation in the inner life and the surrender of the will, be it ever so small a beachhead or so precarious a toehold. To preserve the life from this alien insurgence there is *a Person*, and what a glorious Person! We are now commanded to give no place, room nor opportunity to the devil, (Eph. 4:27). Rather we are to look now to this Person, His glorious conquest and spangled love-banner overhead. We are to consider Him in all the wonders of His being, the marvels of His work, and the authority of His claim upon us. Thus the soul is preserved from collapse, though often under attack, and inspired in the battle to resist the unrelenting foe.

The only hope of victory is to set before the heart, *the place* above and its glorious "things." To appropriate *the power* of the Spirit within. To bring every thought of the mind into the captivity of Christ and to repel the occupation forces of the devil in the realm of the soul, by the exercise of an obedient will, permitting *the glorious Person* of our beloved Lord Jesus, the Captain of our salvation, our Commander, to fully occupy the territory He purchased at such a price on Calvary's cross (Rom. 6:13; 1 Cor. 6:20).

Failure is Not Final

ver feel like giving up? Or have you already done so? Great dreams and noble aspirations of doing a work for God, perhaps on the mission field, have long since dissolved in the harsh light of reality. Now, sitting among the ashes of youthful visions and clothed in the sackcloth of frustrated plans, you consider yourself to be of little use to the Lord. Wait a moment! Remember Barnabas' cousin!

John Mark was raised in fairly well-to-do circumstances. He lived in a roomy house in Jerusalem, set back a little from the main thoroughfare. Unlike the usual city houses, having doors that exited directly on to the street, his had a gateway (Acts 12:12-13). His cousin Barnabas (Col. 4:10 *anepsis,* a cousin) was a leader in the church there, and he was doubtless delighted when taken along with Barnabas and Saul from Jerusalem to Antioch and beyond. What a thrill to be with those two great preachers! Perhaps they would inspire him by their lives to think of becoming a great preacher himself. Content to "carry their Bible bags," he was their "minister." The word literally is "under-rower," a subordinate servant on a ship. This "ship," however, was a *fellow*ship. Not laden with gold of Ophir, but with the riches of God in Christ Jesus, "the gospel to the poor." What young man worth his spiritual salt would not want to be in the company of such men of God? He would hear them pray, preach, discuss the Scriptures, and plan the extension of the work.

But! Ah, those "buts"! All is not well. The golden dreams have lost their glitter. The far-off fields are not as green as they had looked from Jerusalem. Something happens to spoil his vision and sends him home.

What happened? Some suggest it was just plain old homesickness, since he went right home. I doubt that. He was with a close relative, Barnabas, "the son of consolation." Others feel that he was afraid of the rigours of the work and the perils that lay ahead. This seems hard to believe of one to whose birth-name had been added later the name Mark, "the hammer." Still others suggest it was a strong Jewish feeling, moved as he contemplated the inevitable reaching towards the Gentiles. It is inconceivable, however, that as a young man he would consider the great apostle Paul in error.

The problem was serious enough to take him alone back the long journey to Jerusalem, and we can only imagine his teeming thoughts as he went. An issue engendering such strong feelings between godly men of the calibre of Barnabas and Saul as would send them on different ways must have caused much soul distress to those two fellow-workers and their young helper.

Conjecture is no alternative to revelation and we dare not be dogmatic, but an expression in Acts 13:13 may just give us a clue. It reads, "Paul and his company." Previously it had been, "Barnabas and Saul." Now Paul is seen taking the initiative in the case of Bar-Jesus and the miracle of instant blindness on that "child of the devil" (Acts 13:6-11). It seems that Paul has moved into the leadership and Barnabas steps back.

"Paul and his company" indeed! Had Barnabas not been a respected leader in the church at Jerusalem when Saul was a raging fanatic consenting to the death of saints? Was it not his esteemed cousin that took the humbled, newly-converted Paul under his wing and introduced him to the apprehensive saints, speaking for him? "Blood is thicker than water," says the world. How often have family relationships blinded good judgment, and favouritisms hurt harmonious service!

To all intents, young Mark is finished now. His dreams have crashed around him. The center of contention, he returns home and retires from the public eye, as far as the record goes. However, with spiritual men, there is always the fruit of the Spirit to enlarge the heart. While Mark's failure in quitting the work seemed to have set him aside for one aspect of the work, Paul nonetheless recognizes his exercise and appreciates his gift. So we find him commended by Paul to Timothy. "He is profitable to me for the ministry" (2 Tim. 4:11). He also commands his reception without question to the church at Colosse, and calls him, with other fellow-workers, "a comfort." He tells Philemon that Mark is one of his fellow-labourers. Perhaps the most encouraging note in Mark's history is the Lord's approval by using him to pen in extreme simplicity, vivid detail, and forceful style, "The beginning of the gospel of Jesus Christ, the Son of God."

He who is known as an underservant is chosen to portray, in swiftly-moving phrases, the Perfect Servant, as the central Figure in a series of twelve seascapes, six mountain panoramas, five desert scenes, one harvest field picture, three synagogue views, eleven home sketches and three great temple tableaux.

Perhaps this holds a message for some reader—one who has thought that his past failure was final and has spelled *finis* to his usefulness. God may not want you on the mission field, but He may just have a greater work waiting for you.

Standing By

Mary, beautiful and blessed among women, in a special way had yielded herself to God to be the vessel of the incarnation of the Son of God. She had received the twofold promise: she would bear a son, and bear the sword of grief in her own soul.

See her and the other women at the cross now with John. The Saviour of the world is "nailed upon Golgotha's tree." It would appear that the little sorrowing group detached itself from the raucous and unfeeling crowd who mock and take their seat upon the rocks to view the dying agonies of the Man on the middle tree. They take their stand "by" the cross.

There love and loyalty for the rejected and the despised Sufferer is beautifully expressed, though not a word is recorded that they spoke. How can we enter into the feelings of Mary's soul as the promised sword of grief pierces to the innermost cords of her being.

Then we read, "Jesus . . . saw His mother . . . standing by." We can be certain if the suffering Saviour had made but the slightest request of her, she was "standing by," just as available then as when she first heard the angel's startling word at the beginning.

What about the angel? We find the testimony of his position and authority is linked to the very same word. That mighty spirit-being spoke to Zacharias and said, "I am Gabriel, that stand in the presence of God." How long had he stood? An age, a thousand ages? Yet there would be no fidgeting nor impatience as he was standing by in the presence of God. For what? For any command. To be "sent," to "speak," to "show," or just to "stand," it mattered not to that mighty angel. Gabriel just stood silently in the presence of God, available to fulfill the will of God.

What about us? There always seems to be something rather mystical about books and even hymns on "dedication" and "consecration" and "surrendering all." Most of such writings refer or allude to Romans 12:1, "I beseech you therefore, brethren, by the mercies of God, that ye present your bodies a living sacrifice, holy, acceptable unto God, which is your reasonable service." Every earnest believer has faced this verse and perhaps made some sort of offering of oneself to the Lord. That is good. But what is it to "present?" G. Campbell Morgan said, "It is a crisis in the life that becomes a process of living."

Interestingly it is the same word used of Mary and of Gabriel, to "stand." It is not a matter of ability, but availability! There is a great danger that in the assembly we begin to think like the world, evaluate success like the world, and even assess and recognize gift and ability like the world. The world says, "The man on the stage is the star!" Let us never never think that this principle applies in the church, that the man on the platform is the most important gift.

There is no question about the importance of the preaching gifts, but we think like the world when we praise and promote these above other gifts that are not public.

In 1 Corinthians 12, the gifts are likened to members of the body and the point is made that the gifts that are essential to the health of the body are the hidden members. We could do without a hand, if necessary, and still be fit and well, or a limb, but the body cannot survive naturally without a heart, a liver, or lungs. Not beautiful to look at, and certainly not the subject of a photograph to add to the family album as we do with the countenance. But without these . . . nothing.

God is not impressed with ability. He gave it all anyway. But He does delight in availability, since that beautifully reflects His beloved Son.

We shall be forever indebted to godly sisters who for years have breathed our names and our needs into the ear of the Father. We will never forget the living example of all such who displayed the loveliness of Christ and imparted a thirst for holy things. Quiet brethren whose voices are seldom if ever heard in public have blessed us with their discerning wisdom, their shepherd care, their gentle rebuke, their private introduction into the treasure house of the deep things of God.

It seems that far too much promotion is given to the pulpit and not enough encouragement is given to the pulse of the assembly, quietly beating and breathing and bathing the souls of the saints with the elixir of heaven, drawn down in the secret place of prayer and communion with God, by those who are quietly "standing by."

To me remains no place nor time, my country is in every clime,
But with a God to guide our way, 'tis equal joy to go or stay. —Mme. de la Motte Guyon

And Others

Hebrews 11:36-38

Cruel mockings, heartless scourgings,
Bonds and fetid dungeon;
Pounding stones
And dying groans
Of pain, and sorrow surging.

Bodies tortured, spirits tempted,
Clothed in skins; afflicted.
Mountain caves
And lonely graves,
These abject forms have rested.

Regal were they, hearts unearthly,
Heav'ns illustrious army.
That their prayer
And presence share,
This world was all unworthy.

Saint dejected, and rejected
By a world that hates thee;
Christ is nigh,
And to His eye,
Thou'rt fair, belov'd, accepted.

A Psalm for Tough Times

Looking backwards, for many these have been hard times. The state of the economy and worldwide recession have brought hardships and difficulties to not a few. Looking out, we can see the two mightiest nations this world has ever known perfecting and proliferating sophisticated weapons of mass destruction, and we can be sure that these terrifying tools of death were not intended for a military museum! Looking ahead, there is much uncertainty. In the world fear and anxiety abound. For the believer in Christ, however, there are always grounds for joy and themes for praise no matter what our lot may be or what the future holds.

Habakkuk provides for us an inspiring example that it is possible to sing a Psalm of exulting joy even when times are tough. "Habakkuk" means "embracer" and he did embrace by faith what he could not grasp by reason. His message is in the form of a dialogue between himself and the Lord concerning some deep perplexities that assailed him. His little book may be read in five minutes, but its message is for the ages. He had five deep perplexities. Heaven was silent. Iniquity was unchecked. Justice was scorned. The cruel enemy of God's people was raised up to scourge them and God was *seemingly* unfair. Though perplexed and puzzled this man of God took a position of alertness to await an answer and the answer came. Help *will* come, but in God's time and way! *Until then*, life must be lived according to Divine principles and the basis of these is "The just shall live by faith." This principle provides hope in a dark day and is timeless. It is picked up in the New Testament and given to the Romans. There the emphasis is on the JUST. It is sent to the Galatians and there the emphasis is on the LIFE. It seals the epistle to the Hebrews and there the emphasis is on the FAITH.

The earthling turns to artificial means in times of distress. In chapter 2, we see them resorting to drink and giving others to drink. This is truly the "spirit" of the age. Whatever goes wrong, for many their answer is alcohol. If it is a celebration "Let's drink to that." If it is a shock "Have a drink, it'll steady your nerves." If it is a crisis to face, "Have a stiff drink." If it is a sorrow to bear "Let me pour you a drink." Immorality and idolatry followed in Habakkuk's day as it does today. But God condemns the futility of such means of escape as lifeless lies and He commands their babblings to be silenced.

The child of God however has a different life principle. It is to face the realities of life by faith in a Mighty Helper. Instead of being silent, the believer has the liberty to enter the holy place by the prayer of faith. So Habakkuk does, and what a prayer! In spite of how things appear, his prayer is no grumbling dirge. It is accompanied by an exulting spirit. He has his priorities right. No matter what should happen to him, he longs for the prosperity of the Lord's work. He takes his language from Scripture by echoing the words of Moses and the victorious song of Deborah. He embraced by faith the inspired Word. Even though he himself was in the dark, the brightness of God's glory and the resources of His power were not diminished. He is the Sovereign Lord over the forces of nature, the might of the nations and the power of the enemy. Things often get out of our control, but we can exult with Habakkuk, that nothing ever gets out of His. Therefore, the believer lives by faith and sings when times are tough.

In spite of recession there can be rejoicing. Habakkuk had two reasons for exulting joy. The God of his Salvation and the Salvation of his God. What glorious songs have come from the pens of saints down through the ages concerning those grand subjects and often out of deep trial. He sings of his God as the Source and the Sphere of his joy in spite of deep deprivation of fragrance, fruit, food and flock. Enjoyment and employment were gone and on top of that his life was in danger. What to do? Escape? Withdraw? Complain? No! He cleared his throat and sang! He sang about his God and about the salvation of his God! Grand subjects for any song.

Dear reader, past pleasures and luxuries may be gone for a season. Hardships may lie upon you and may yet increase. Oh, there is great therapy in a song of praise to God and joy in His salvation. You can think of some! "O God of Matchless Grace, we sing unto Thy Name . . ." How about that one to begin with? Or, "O God, our help in ages past, Our hope for years to come"? Dust off the hymn book and clear those vocal cords and try it today. They may crackle a bit and the tune may be a bit off key but let us give evidence that having been dug out of the pit we do have something . . . yea, *Someone* to sing about!

His Majesty

A small business envelope arrived in the early days of the war. Not much to look at. No decoration graced it, no floral design relieved it. Certainly no perfume promised a letter of love within. For all who received one like it they will not forget it for their lives would never again be the same. Apart from the name and address of the recipient the only other printing was brief, stark, bold. In the corner were just the letters "O H M S." It was an order to report for military service.

It meant separation of loved ones, upheavals, danger and for some, wounding and death. Why then did the recipients answer such a call? Why not ignore it? "O H M S" that's why! Those initials stood for "On His Majesty's Service." Behind that plain envelope and brusque command lay all the authority of the British Crown. To obey meant dangers but to disobey meant the retribution of the law.

We live in a different day now. The sense of majesty is all but gone. The spirit of a casual world tends to overspill into the church. It is not just the problem of sloppy appearance, scruffy decorum and chummy language with God. These are but the symptoms of a deeper disorder, the departure from the sense of "His Majesty." This is an inner state, a fixed attitude brought in from a world that despises dominions and speaks evil of dignities (Jude 1:8).

A number of words in both Old and New Testaments are translated, "Majesty." They are used to convey such ideas as "magnificence," "splendour," "glory," "beauty," "excelling," "honour," "to rise up," "increase," "triumph," "greatness."

There was majesty in the court of Nebuchadnezzar. It was displayed in the absolute rule of the king over the lives of his subjects. There was majesty in the court of Ahasuerus so that none could enter the king's presence without his permission, on pain of death. There was such majesty in the court of Solomon that a great queen was quite overcome in her spirit. However, all the majesties of earth must fade as a shadow before "the glory of His majesty" who is God over all blessed forever.

This is called "the majesty in the heavens." Job was instructed by God about this majesty by the flashings of lightning and the rolling of thunder. He was directed to view the vast blue vault of space, to consider the uncontrollable wind. The invisible foundations of the earth and the visible host of the night sky are all called to declare the majesty of God. Waves of the sea, treasures of snow, radiance of light and marvels of nature are all witnesses of the greatness of the majesty of God.

When Isaiah saw it, he cried, "Woe is me." When John saw it he fell as a dead man. The blaze of it blinded Saul of Tarsus on the Damascus turnpike and laid him on the ground.

"But," objects someone, "we live in a day of grace." Another says, "God is our Father and we are His children and perfect love casts out fear." Well, we will not for the moment discuss who among us has "perfect love" but in our delight in the lowliness of the Lamb of God we are apt to forget His loftiness as the Lord of Glory. We have confused the joys of intimacy with the arrogance of familiarity with God. We fail to distinguish between His goodness and His holiness, His love and His justice, His grace and His truth, His beneficence and His magnificence.

We are apt to forget in moments of honeyed sentiment that a great deal has happened since the Son of man had nowhere to lay His head. He is not now "Jesus only." "God hath made that same Jesus both Lord and Christ." We shall ever delight in that precious saving Name of Jesus, but when with unshod feet and chastened spirit we draw near to His Majesty, let us not hesitate to glorify Him by ascribing His Lordly title and anointed ministry.

Do we know God more intimately than Abraham, David, Daniel or Isaiah? Are we closer to the Master than was Peter, John, or Paul? Do we commune with the Father more intimately than the Son? Then by what measure do we think we may use the common language of equals in the august presence of Him from before whose face mountains melt and worlds collapse? Or is it that we have created a god after our own image from our own religious imagination and breathed into this deity of dust the breath of our own ingenuity. Thus we need feel no holy awe nor hold a sense of majesty nor ever learn to be silent in prostrate wonder before HIS MAJESTY!

Majestic sweetness sits enthroned upon the Saviour's brow;
His head with radiant glories crowned, His lips with grace o'erflow. —Samuel Stennett

Look Up

Abraham is one of the greatest figures ever to cross the page of human history. While the kings of the east and the Pharaohs of Egypt have long since moldered in the memories of men, this man from Ur of the Chaldees remains a majestic figure esteemed and revered by millions. What marks this man out above many? What made him great?

There are some things that many have considered important in their striving for greatness. Riches rank high on the list. Influence is another. Military superiority has been for many their goal of greatness. Of Abram it is recorded "he was very rich in cattle, in silver, and in gold." This man had influence with men, with cities and with God Himself. In battle, Abram fought with a small commando force of 318 men and scored a decisive victory against the armies of four kings. Yet for all this it was not his wealth, influence not military prowess that contributed to his greatness. We read instead, in Romans 4:20 that he "was strong in faith, giving glory to God."

There was something missing in the life of this man and his wife Sarai however. The prattle of an infant and the laughter of a child had never blessed their home nor gladdened their hearts. They were childless. Then the Lord gave him the promise of a land and of a seed that would be as numberless as the dust of the earth.

Still the years rolled on and old age seemed to carry away with it the possibility of ever having a child. More than riches, more than influence, more than power, his great longing was for a son to be his rightful heir. Abram must learn that *God's delays are not necessarily His denials.* God's timing is always just right. He is never too soon nor too late.

The word of the Lord came again, assuring Abram of the certainty of the Divine promise. The Lord brought him out under the night sky to give him now the promise of a heavenly progeny with spiritual blessings of which Abraham would be known as "the father of the faithful."

It seems, however, that there was even more in those words, "Look now toward heaven . . . ." There was no hope within, no help beneath. If there was going to be a new beginning, a new life, it would have to come from above.

For many life seems so far gone. The dreams of youth have faded in the mists of ponderous years. Hope has foundered on the rocks of utter disappointment, all seems gone. The promise of God so long ago seems, like Abram's name ("father of elevation"), to mock them. Now the Lord would speak again assuring all such that there is hope. Not from within, for naturally we are like Abram, "as good as dead." Not from beneath, for no power nor wisdom of man can provide the needed help.

Hear the word of the Lord today, "Look now toward heaven!" All else may have failed. Dearest friends, nearest loved ones, closest companions, personal resources all may be gone. "LOOK NOW TOWARD HEAVEN!"

Remember that for us in our day there is a Man in the Glory: "Jesus Christ who is gone into heaven, and is on the right hand of God; angels and authorities and powers being made subject unto Him" (1 Peter 3:22). He is willing and able to give the promised help. He is only waiting until we turn to Him.

What Abram did was noteworthy: "He believed in the Lord." What he did *not* do is well worth noting also. In Romans 4:19, *he considered not the immensity of the problem!* His own body as good as dead. How often do we wonder HOW God can accomplish the seeming impossible, as we recognize our human limitations. Abram did not question "How?" Then *he staggered not at the immensity of the promise!* How often do we view the vastness of the Divine promise and faint. Abram did not try to number either the dust or the stars. He just took God at His Word. The immensity of the promise did not stagger him. He could not understand it, but he believed in the God who made it. *He doubted not the immensity of the power* that could fulfill the promise. The God who could sprinkle the heavens with a starry host without number and uphold them all in harmonious magnificence can certainly do what He had promised. Thus mingling his faith with his hope Abram has this testimony, that he "was strong in faith, giving glory to God."

Troubled soul, weary servant, shattered sufferer, lonely believer, "LOOK NOW TOWARD HEAVEN."

Fellowship With God

"Truly our fellowship, is with the Father and with His Son, Jesus Christ."

To "walk with God" Is this some dreamer's dream,
Reserved for ancient men of different cast
Than I? For men of slowly moving years?
And must I think such holy joy is past?

And can it be, that as from distant Ur,
There is a path that leads from idol shrine,
Marked out by tent, by altar and by fire,
Yet points me to the glory that is Thine?

And is it so, that I may walk with Thee?
May hear Thy voice above earth's din below?
And like old Sinai's sage and warrior saint,
May find Thy ways and see Thine afterglow?

How can I see Invisibility?
Or how with finite mind reach to confide
Transcendent thoughts; or how with halting thigh
Draw near, and keep apace Thy mighty stride?

A mystery? There is a Way for all
Who thirst for God; not trod by feet, but heart;
An eye, not needing man's external aids;
A mind, the schools of earth cannot impart.

"The Way," to reach the Inaccessible.
"The Truth," the great Inscrutable to know.
"The Life"; And thus He opens up the eye
To see—the mind to grasp—the way to go.

To "walk with God"? 'Tis not too late to join
That holy band, who soared above the sod
Of transient things—of weights—besetting sin,
And feel the mighty pulse of life with God.

The Beginning of Blessing

It was a beautiful day in the fall of the year. The trees wore their golden regalia with dignity. But it was turning cold. Soon, cumulo-nimbus giants were roiling in the distance, pushing their turrets ever higher till the altitude flattened their tops into the classic anvil head of the massive storm-cloud. It was too early for snow, the trees were still loaded with leaves and fruit. Too soon they came, a few flakes spinning down to tell us more were on the way. Sure enough, down it fell, in large feathery deposits that quickly covered the ground and began to fill the trees.

Next morning we awoke to a dazzling display of winter's artistry. Then we saw it! A young maple tree on the front lawn that had looked so bright and straight yesterday in the sun. The trunk was split right to the ground. It had capitulated to the weight of the snow on the leaves. I had never seen such a thing before. That beautiful tree found the burden too heavy and there it lay as though in an agony, torn apart.

I have often complained at the brevity of the glorious fall, so soon it is swept away into winter by the winds and heavy rains that tear the leaves from every branch. That day, perhaps I understood a little more about the order of things. From a lesson of the broken tree I learned that the leaves must be stripped away, or else the trees would be broken under the weight of the snow.

The stark branches of the winter trees, colourless and bare, have as much beauty as a skeleton. But they can bear the weight of the snow and let the storm whistle through their unlovely frame, bending and yielding to its blast. It waits for the return of spring when the sap will flow and life burst forth in bud and blossom as the root draws from the earth sweetened by the winter snows.

Before the Lord Jesus went to the cross, He spent that memorable time alone with His disciples, mostly in the upper room. He showed them a living parable of His unfinished work "out of this world" on their behalf. He unfolded to them visions of glory beyond Golgotha's gloom. How they needed that as they approached the sorrows of the next few days.

As He introduced them to the ministry of the Holy Spirit that would follow, He said, "I have yet many things to say unto you, but ye cannot bear them now" (Jn. 16:12). For the word "bear" He uses an unusual verb. It is the bearing of a burden. A full revelation of the cross and its mighty significance would be just too much for them at that time. Trembling and fearful and full of questions, as they were then, they would have broken under it. They must pass through the winter dark first, when the sun refused to shine, and feel that they have lost everything precious to them. All their Treasure, their peace and hope would be nailed on a cross and torn from them and they themselves would learn something of that blasting storm in their own lives.

As Jacob discovered after the night of wrestling, their sun would shine again. The Lord would rise and hope would spring up. Life would surge into their barren souls again. Then by the Spirit's power there would be fruit and flower, joy and rejoicing as they, strengthened with might in the inner man would learn that their Beloved Lord was dwelling in their hearts by faith. They would reach out to apprehend the vastness of the love of Christ, and within, be "filled with all the fullness of God."

God will never pour an ocean of blessing into an unprepared heart. He will always develop the vessel to contain the suited blessing. Otherwise, the blessing would only be a burden too heavy to bear.

Dear puzzled believer, follower of Christ, ever seeking God's highest gifts and noblest benefits, you have prayed great prayers, sought mighty treasures from His Word. Instead, has come the blast of winter winds stripping you of your beauty and leaving the soul stark in your sorrowing night and you cry an anguished "Why?" into the dark.

Faint not, beloved! God has heard your great prayers. The answer is on the way, but first you must be strengthened with might by His Spirit in the inner man to bear the freight of blessings you have sought. The stripping is the beginning of blessing!

You may not look as beautiful as once you were. You may no longer be praised in the sunlight as others seem to be. But God's hand has been on you, His storms have prepared you, He has stripped away your own glory, the deadwood is broken off. Soon the mighty sap of the Spirit's power will flow. God will keep His promise and many will bless the Lord that through your sorrows He has prepared you to be a channel of blessing to many and to glorify Him in your body and in your spirit.

"Oft we shrink from the purging and pruning, forgetting the Husbandman knows
That the deeper the cutting and paring, the richer the cluster that grows."